Liberation Theology
for Armchair Theologians

Also available in the Armchair Theologians series

Aquinas for Armchair Theologians by Timothy M. Renick
Augustine for Armchair Theologians by Stephen A. Cooper
Barth for Armchair Theologians by John R. Franke
Bonhoeffer for Armchair Theologians by Stephen R. Haynes and Lori Brandt Hale
Calvin for Armchair Theologians by Christopher Elwood
Heretics for Armchair Theologians by Justo L. Gonzalez and Catherine Gunsalus Gonzalez
Jonathan Edwards for Armchair Theologians by James P. Byrd
John Knox for Armchair Theologians by Suzanne McDonald
Luther for Armchair Theologians by Steven Paulson
Martin Luther King Jr. for Armchair Theologians by Rufus Burrow Jr.
The Reformation for Armchair Theologians by Glenn S. Sunshine
Wesley for Armchair Theologians by William J. Abraham

Liberation Theology
for Armchair Theologians

MIGUEL A. DE LA TORRE

ILLUSTRATIONS BY RON HILL

WESTMINSTER
JOHN KNOX PRESS
LOUISVILLE · KENTUCKY

First edition
Published by Westminster John Knox Press
Louisville, Kentucky

13 14 15 16 17 18 19 20 21 22—10 9 8 7 6 5 4 3 2 1

Unless otherwise indicated, Scripture quotations
are the author's own translation.

Book design by Sharon Adams
Cover design by Jennifer K. Cox
Cover illustration: Ron Hill

Library of Congress Cataloging-in-Publication Data

De La Torre, Miguel A.
 Liberation theology for armchair theologians / Miguel De La
Torre ; illustrations by Ron Hill. — First [edition].
   pages cm. — (Armchair theologians series)
 Includes bibliographical references and index.
 ISBN 978-0-664-23813-1 (alk. paper)
 1. Liberation theology. I. Title.
 BT83.57.D4 2013
 230'.0464—dc23

                                                    2013019812

♾ The paper used in this publication meets the minimum requirements
of the American National Standard for Information Sciences—
Permanence of Paper for Printed Library Materials, ANSI Z39.48-1992.

Most Westminster John Knox Press books are available at special
quantity discounts when purchased in bulk by corporations,
organizations, and special-interest groups. For more information,
please e-mail SpecialSales@wjkbooks.com.

To
those who are misinformed
about liberation theology

Contents

Preface and Acknowledgments   ix

1. Resistance!   1

2. Opening the Windows   21

3. Liberation Theologies: What Are They?   41

4. Early Proponents   63

5. Liberation in *El Norte*   85

6. The Faiths of the People   113

7. Moving beyond Liberation Theology   141

Notes   153

For Further Reading   157

Index   161

Preface
and Acknowledgments

I am amazed at the misinformation surrounding liberation theology. Both the theology and the religious movement associated with it have been demonized by religious institutions (including churches), the media, and governments. To have theological disagreements would not warrant much concern if it were not for the fact that multitudes throughout the world who have expounded liberative theological thoughts have been killed or have disappeared. What is it about liberation theology that has led many to their graves? Why is this theological perspective deemed so dangerous? Why have governments, including that of the United States, committed so many resources to bring about its obliteration? Not since the Roman persecutions of the early Christian church have large numbers of believers in Christ been so frequently martyred by the state for holding a particular theological perspective.

No doubt, the strong negative reaction against the many manifestations of liberation theology by the privileged and powerful indicates its revolutionary nature. But liberation theology is not revolutionary as that term is usually defined by our society. What makes liberation theology truly radical is its focus on the poor, the marginalized, the dispossessed, and the disenfranchised. While most theologies are developed by religious leaders and academicians, liberation theology attempts to reflect upon the divine as understood from the underside of history. In it, the everyday trials and tribulations of the voiceless become the source for the voice of God.

Liberation theology is so dangerous because it disrupts a religious and political worldview that supports social structures that privilege the few at the expense of the many. Ignorance of the causes of oppression is crucial to maintaining this worldview. But as the consciousness of the oppressed begins to be raised, as they begin to see with their own eyes that their repressive conditions are contrary to the will of God, the power and privilege of the few who benefit from the status quo is threatened. For this reason, liberationist theological thought must be suppressed, by whatever means necessary.

One of the most effective ways to combat liberationist theological thought is through misinformation. For this reason, a short introduction to the theology and movement—such as the book you hold in your hands—is important. My motive in writing this book was to combat the misunderstanding surrounding liberation theology, but I have found that writing for the Armchair series has been a personally fulfilling process. I am grateful to the series editor, Don McKim, for the invitation to participate. Also, I wish to thank my administrative assistant, Debbie McLean, who proofread these pages, and my research assistants, Becky Chabot and Sarah Neeley, who proofread the final galleys. And if it wasn't for the love and support I receive from my wife, Deb, none of my books would have been possible.

CHAPTER ONE

Resistance!

Wherever oppression resides, one can also find resistance. This resistance, this cry for freedom, uttered from the depths of the inhuman condition in which vast segments of the world's population have been forced to live throughout history, becomes a cry that Christian churches must hear if they wish to remain faithful to the good news. For Christians, Jesus came so that all can have life and have it abundantly (John 10:10). Any theology that instead brings or is complicit with death is by definition satanic. The promise of the abundant life is not for some messianic future; it is for the here and now. Yet as we read news reports filled with stories of decimation, discrimination, disenfranchisement, and dispossession, we are left wondering where this abundant life is that our faith promises.

Jesus' promise of an abundant life remains beyond the grasp of most of the earth's people due in part to a disproportionate distribution of natural resources. The globalization of the economy, coupled with the military strength of a few nations (especially the United States), ensures and maintains a continual flow of cheap labor and raw materials to a privileged minority of the world's population. Not surprisingly, the rich get fewer yet wealthier, while the poor continue to grow as they slip into greater poverty. Ironically, those who benefit from these arrangements have constructed a type of Christianity that justifies global structures responsible for much of the world's economic misery.

Any armchair historian knows that our Christian story is full of atrocities committed in the name of Jesus. From the inquisition to witch burnings, from the crusades to the colonial ventures of civilizing and Christianizing the so-called heathens, the story of our faith is one of imposing oppressive structures to force others to believe and accept the same doctrines that justify the power and privilege of whatever culture is ruling. All too often, churches have stood in solidarity with the presiding political powers to carve an influential space for themselves in the nation's public arena.

From the underside of what has been considered normative, however, a cry of resistance can be heard echoing through the pages of history. We can hear this cry lifted up by some of the early church fathers who, in solidarity with the poor, portrayed wealth as an impediment to salvation. They insisted that those who possessed riches had a moral obligation toward the poor. To ignore the poor bordered on idolatry, replacing materialism for spirituality. As the

second-century theologian and martyr Polycarp said, "If anyone does not refrain from the love of money he will be defiled by idolatry and so be judged as if he was one of the heathen, 'who are ignorant of the judgment of the Lord.'"[1] We can continue to follow this thread of seeking solidarity with the least of these in the actions of a medieval bishop of Paris, Guillaume d'Auxerre, who, along with other theologians living during the plagues and famine of the twelfth and thirteenth centuries, insisted that the poor were not sinning if they engaged in "starvation theft." In fact, the poor had a right to steal what they needed in order to survive. This cry against the systematic economic forces that cause oppression can also be heard in the mystical prayers of the fourteenth-century Dominican nun, Catherine of Siena. Writing against the wealthy of her time and the social structures they constructed to enrich themselves, she asked,

3

"How can these wretched evil people share their possessions with the poor when they are already stealing from them?"[2]

It would be simplistic and unscholarly to impose the modern term *liberation theologian* upon such historical figures as Polycarp, Guillaume d'Auxerre, or Catherine of Siena. Still, we can say that these historical figures, and others like them, expressed liberationist ideals. Their understanding of Christianity led them to believe that the universal church of Jesus Christ had a moral obligation to stand in solidarity with those marginalized by the secular and ecclesiastical social structures of their day. During those times when the church appeared to be aligned more with the interests of the ruling and economically privileged classes, women and men of faith searched deep within their religious tradition to formulate a practical and spiritual response to the causes of poverty and oppression.

Obviously, this modern concept of liberation was not created *ex nihilo*, out of nothing. The historical trend of faithful servants of God resisting the powers and principalities of this world became the antecedent to what would come to be known in Latin America during the 1960s as liberation theology. In fact, we can say that any spiritual movements (not just Christian ones) that seek to dismantle the social structures responsible for the creation of poverty and oppression are liberative. It is important here to distinguish between liberation theology and liberative theologies. Liberation theology is rooted within the Christian faith, while liberative theologies need not be Christian. As we will see later, liberative religious movements can be Muslim, Hindu, or even humanist. Although our focus will remain on liberationist-type theologies emanating from Christian sources, a chapter will also explore other religious liberative theological movements.

Origins of Liberation Theology

A countertradition of resistance rooted in the plight of the oppressed has always existed within the Christian faith. For the purposes of this book, we will focus on the development of this liberationist countertradition in the Americas, even though this trend can be traced to the start of the Christian faith, if not before. This liberationist spirit arose in the Western hemisphere among those whom the Christian conquistadores considered savages and heathens. We can pinpoint the start of this liberationist movement in the so-called New World to January 13, 1493, for on that day, Native American blood first flowed—a prelude to one of the most notorious genocides human history has ever witnessed.

As Christians hunted down Indian men as if they were dogs, as Indian women were being raped, and as Indian children were being disemboweled, a voice of resistance arose in the form of a *cacique*, a chieftain, by the name of Hatuey. Creating a loose confederation of Taíno Caribbean Indians to resist the invading European colonizers, Hatuey carried out a style of guerrilla warfare against the invading Christian Spaniards. This renegade chieftain was eventually captured and condemned to death as an example to others. As Hatuey was about to be burned at the stake, a Franciscan friar attempted to convert him to the Christian faith, with the promise of heaven and the threat of hell. Prior to setting the fire that would burn the Indian leader alive, the friar promised mercy in the form of strangulation. Hatuey asked that if he accepted Christianity would he go to heaven, and if he did, would he find Christians there. "Of course," the friar replied, to which the condemned warrior retorted that he did not want to go anyplace where he would be forced to be with such cruel people as Christians. Although Hatuey was not a Christian, he is probably the first liberative figure to resist the conquest of the Americas by European Christians.

Establishing a Colonial Christendom

Hatuey and many others like him stood in solidarity with the subjugated by struggling against the forces responsible for systematic oppression, even when those forces included the Christian church. The Roman Catholic Church played a prominent role in the colonial venture, as did North American Protestant churches in later years. For the enslavement and genocide of the indigenous people to take place, the religious conquistadores required philosophical, theological, and scientific justification. By questioning if

Indians even had souls, clerics and conquistadores were able to divide among themselves the land, riches, labor, and precious resources used by the original inhabitants.

Shortly after a lost Columbus was discovered by the indigenous people of the Caribbean, a weakened Vatican under Pope Alexander VI (the former Rodrigo Lanzol Borja from Spain) sped up the colonial venture in 1494 by entrusting all ecclesiastical powers operating in what was then called New Spain to the Spanish crown. Through *patronato real* (the king's patronage), the king was given the right to appoint individuals to the high ecclesiastical offices and to administer the tithes. In effect, the king of Spain became a vice pope, appointing bishops whose first

7

allegiance was to the crown rather than the cross. Hence, the Catholic Church, having been complicit with the powers responsible for the dispossession of the Indians, became closely aligned with the political structures and dependent upon them to exercise influence over the masses. The Church provided the crown with religious legitimacy in its actions against the indigenous inhabitants of the land; in return, the crown provided the church with a space from which to operate. Together, the cross and the sword plundered and decimated the indigenous population.

Spanish and Portuguese saw themselves as elected by God, called to what was for them a "new world" full of opportunities. They were possessed with a religious fervor to convert the so-called heathens, by the sword if necessary, and a materialist fever to take away their lands, possessions, and labor. Conquistador Hernán Cortés probably said it best: "We come to serve God and King, and also to get gold."[3] The prospects of gold and glory led conquistadores to move beyond the islands of the Caribbean and toward the mainland. Soon, mighty indigenous political structures such as the Aztec, Mayan, and Incan empires succumbed to the military superiority of the colonizers and the diseases they brought with them. The indigenous populations faced humiliating servitude and decimation.

What was established in the so-called new world was a feudal Iberian political system merged with a medieval church of those who understood their mission in the Americas as a continued crusade to eradicate nonbelievers from their presence. In the minds of the colonizers, Spain's political goals became synonymous with Christ's mission. For over 700 years, the Islamic Moors ruled on the Iberian Peninsula. Although there existed periods of relative peace between Muslims, Jews, and Christians, a continual crusade by Christians against Muslim and Jewish "infidels" always

existed under the surface and at times emerged in the form of violence and war. During these 700 years of Muslim rule, a militant form of Christianity was forged. In the same year that Columbus arrived in the Caribbean, the victorious Christians of Spain gave their Muslim and Jewish neighbors an ultimatum: convert or be expatriated. It was this crusading spirit that was imported to the Western Hemisphere.

On the underside of Christendom, an unofficial church of resistance was established in the Americas. Priests of various religious orders stood in solidarity with Indians. Their vows of poverty made it possible for these clerics to live and struggle with the oppressed. What developed was a two-tiered, informal ecclesiastical structure. On the top were the official representatives of Christendom, agents of and for the colonialists. At their underside were those who represented the plight of the marginalized and outcasts. Clerics such as Bartolomé de Las Casas (1484–1566), Antonio Montesinos (1486–1540), Diego de Medellín (1496–1593), Antonio de Valdivieso (d. 1549), and Juan del Valle (d. 1561) saw those occupying this underside as the true church. Because clerics such as these preached against the inhumanity faced by the natives and promoted resistance to oppressive policies, many modern-day liberationist theologians see them as the forerunners to what would become Latin American liberation theology. Unfortunately, many of these clerics who stood in solidarity with the "least of these" still held to the prevailing worldview that the disenfranchised were like ignorant children in need of Christian tutelage.

Bartolomé de Las Casas

Liberation theologian Gustavo Gutiérrez states: "Among those with the keenest interest in Bartolomé de Las Casas today are Latin America's liberation theologians, who have recognized in the Dominican friar a prophetic forerunner of the church's radical 'option for the poor.'"[4] Las Casas arrived in Santo Domingo in 1514 and was given an *encomienda*. The *encomienda* was a labor system employed by the conquistadores in which the Spanish crown granted to an individual both land and native people. The grantee of the *encomienda* was responsible for protecting the Indians from warring tribes and teaching them the ways of Christianity and Spanish "civilization," including the language. In return, the natives were to provide tribute to the grantee of the *encomienda* in the form of labor, crops, or precious metals.

Las Casas eventually renounced his riches and slaves, joined the Dominican order, and dedicated his life to seeking justice for Indians. For his remaining fifty years, Las Casas devoted himself to their struggle, standing in solidarity with them as they fought the Spanish authorities for liberation from conquest. Called to be a witness of Christ to

the "godless" Indians, Las Casas soon realized that it was he, the priest and missionary, who was living without God. Las Casas concluded that conversion could not be defined as accepting some theological proposition; rather, conversion had to be based on actions taken. To be converted to Christ meant being converted through the Christlike liberative actions in which one engaged. The actions of Las Casas, including his ownership of several indigenous people as slaves, gave witness that it was he who was rejecting the message of the gospel. In short, it was he who was in need of conversion.

Because Las Casas equated salvation with the establishment of social justice, the unjust treatment of the Indians by the hands of Spaniards placed the conquistadores' salvation

in jeopardy. Salvation could not be reduced to a profession of faith, for after all, Las Casas had lived his life professing Christianity. Salvation had to be linked to how Jesus Christ was understood. For Las Casas, and the liberationist theologians who would follow, Jesus Christ was the "least of these," the one suffering hunger, thirst, nakedness, alienation, infirmity, and incarceration (Matt. 7:21–27). Conversion became the process by which one came to know Christ as one of the disenfranchised, and the action one took in developing a lifestyle of solidarity with the marginalized. For Las Casas, Christ could be found among the Indians because of their oppression, not because of any profession of faith that they might have made. If the Spaniards wanted to find Christ, they needed to look to the Indians they were massacring.

Hence, in the writings of Las Casas, Indians are not pagans, natural slaves, or wild children of nature. They are humans with the capacity for salvation, regardless of the conquistadores' assertion that they were soulless, human-looking, talking animals. The Christian conquerors might have defined Indians like Hatuey as "unbelievers"; nevertheless, the Indians' humanity made them sacred because they contained the *imago Dei*, the image of God. They represented the poor of the gospel, and as such, any gesture made to them was a gesture made toward Christ. To mistreat the native people was to mistreat Jesus. To look into these poor, marginalized, and suffering faces was to recognize the suffering of Christ. To establish power and privilege at the expense of the indigenous populations was to make a mockery of Christ's blood, which was shed in solidarity with the wretched of the earth. Hence, salvation for Las Casas meant crucifying the power and privilege derived from owning an *encomienda*, so that he could authentically accompany Christ in the struggle to liberate the Indians. The *encomienda* system finally ended in the eighteenth century, not due to any theological considerations, but because the economic need of Spain to strengthen its military meant that less of the tributes from the work of the Indians were left for the *criollos* (children of the conquistadores born in the Americas).

Las Casas's praxis in attempting to stand in solidarity with the Indians against the genocide they faced earned him the title "Protector of the Indians." Yet there are those, such as Native American scholar George "Tink" Tinker, who insist that Las Casas "was in the final analysis thoroughly committed to european colonialism and the exploitation of Indian lands and labor. His concession to his christian conscience was to promulgate 'a greater conquest' conducted by the church on behalf of his royal majesties in Spain."[5] For Tinker, even though Las Casas worked to "protect" the Indians from bodily genocide, he was still complicit in cultural genocide, attempting to destroy indigenous culture and replace it with a "european-centered" value system.

The Rise of Latin America

The Latin American society that Christendom had a hand in creating was divided along strict class lines. At the top of the hierarchy were those born in Spain. They were known as *peninsulares* and mainly occupied top leadership positions within the colonial government and the church. Below them were their offspring born in the colonies. They were

referred to as *criollos*. As second-class citizens, they mostly filled government positions. Below them were the urban white masses, then Indians, and then at the bottom of the social ladder, *mestizos* (offspring of natives and whites), *mulatos* (offspring of blacks and whites), and Africans, along with their descendants.

The early 1800s saw the rise of Latin American nationalistic fervor and the resulting wars for independence, helped in part by Napoleon's 1807 occupation of Spain. The emerging nations sought to maintain the same control over the church that Spain previously held. At the forefront was Christendom, the space carved out by the royal ruling power, which in turn provided religious legitimacy to the existing social structures. Christendom, according to Pablo Richard, shaped a church that bore the marks of slavery, oppression, dependency, and underdevelopment; thus contributing to the colonizing process. For liberation to occur, for the church to be born, Christendom must die.[6] Not surprisingly, when local elites started the wars for independence, the church, because it was usually the largest landholder and the main conservative political force, was perceived to be an enemy. Even though some priests of the lower clergy cast their lots with the revolutionaries (for example Miguel Hidalgo y Costilla in Mexico), most local bishops sided with the Spanish crown, while popes made proclamations against independence movements in 1816 and 1823.

The poor and dispossessed took up arms in the struggle for independence; however, when the fog of war cleared, their plight was not altered. Rather than the crown and the church, they were now subjugated to the commercial class and local landholders. With victory came laws confiscating the land of those whom the local elites viewed as backward, specifically the lands of the church, religious orders, and

Indians. Over time, the church aligned itself with the interests of the landowning class to counter the rise in the late 1800s of the Liberals, with their pro-European, anticlerical Enlightenment views. Even though independence had been declared, Latin America soon found itself dependent on the economic power first of the British Empire, and then of the United States. This economic subjugation created the conditions throughout Latin America, and especially Central America, that would give rise to liberationist theologies.

Bananas

Before 1870, most Americans had never heard of bananas. In that year, and working independently of each other, Lorenzo Dow Baker and Minor Keith introduced bananas to the American consumer. Within a decade, Americans had gone bananas over bananas. The prospects of tremendous profits led Baker and Keith, along with Andrew Preston, to join forces in 1890 to create the Boston Fruit Company. By 1899, Americans were consuming over 16 million bunches a year. That was also the year that Boston Fruit merged with United Fruit to create the notorious United Fruit Company, the largest banana company in the world, with plantations throughout Central America, South America, and the Caribbean.

Around this time, President Theodore Roosevelt started talking about "speaking softly but carrying a big stick" and practicing what came to be known as "gun-boat diplomacy." The result was to place the full force of the U.S. military at the disposal of U.S. corporations such as the United Fruit Company to protect their business interests. For example, when Manuel Estrada Cabrera, the Guatemalan dictator, gave the United Fruit Company free reign in 1901 to own land for growing bananas, the U.S. military

made sure that the company's interests remained well protected. Guatemala's subjugation to U.S. corporate interests (hence the term "banana republic") was not limited to Guatemala; every nation within the Caribbean basin (along with several South American countries) were economically and politically subject to U.S. corporate and political interests, even to the point where countries were unable to choose their own leader without the expressed blessings of the U.S. ambassador to that country.

By the 1950s, 70 percent of the land in Guatemala was controlled by 2.2 percent of the population, with only 10 percent of the land available to 90 percent of the mostly Indian population. Most of the land was unused. When Jacobo Arbenz was elected president through a free and open contest, he implemented modest land reforms to deal with this injustice. However, he ran into one major problem: the United Fruit Company was a major holder of unused land. Not surprisingly, the Eisenhower administration covertly overthrew the democratically elected government of Arbenz and replaced it with a military dictatorship under the pretense that Arbenz was a communist. This led to continuous political unrest over the next thirty years, and hundreds of thousands of people died or disappeared.

Again, U.S. intervention was not limited to Guatemala. During the twentieth century, eleven countries bordering the Caribbean experienced some twenty-one military invasions and twenty-six covert CIA operations whose purpose was to topple their governments, or what we euphemistically call today "regime change."

¡Basta! (Enough!)

Every so often the poor, the marginalized, and the disenfranchised have had enough. The threat of death that has for generations kept them submissive to the overarching economic and political structures loses its power. They demand change, they demand liberation—regardless of personal cost or sacrifice. In recent history, such moments include the civil rights movement of the 1950s and 1960s in the United States, the 1968 Prague Spring in Czechoslovakia, the 1989 Autumn of Nations in the former Eastern European bloc, the 1989 Tiananmen Square protests in China, and the 2011 Jasmine Revolution that swept Northern Africa and the Middle East. As people yearn to breathe free, the question remains: What role does the church play? Will clerics stand with the state that oppresses its people, as Christendom has done? Or will clerics stand in solidarity with the oppressed, sharing their fate of dying or

disappearing? Religion can either fulfill the prophecy uttered by Karl Marx and become the opiate of the people, a narcotic that numbs the oppressed to the reality of their sufferings through promises of riches in some future heaven after they die, or religion can raise consciousness.

Liberation theology is a faith that raises consciousness. The historical role Christendom has played on behalf of the state is to convince the masses that they are not the victims of unjust social structures. Rather than religion paternalistically encouraging lethargy and ignorance so that people remain obedient and dependent on political, economic, and social dominance, liberation theology strives to raise critical awareness concerning the unholy causes of oppression. It is a radical manifestation of faith that believes in Jesus' promise of an abundant life, and anything that prevents people from realizing this promise in their lives is not from God, whether it be the state or the church.

19

This abundant life, this humanization, is not limited to those who are oppressed, however; it is also for the oppressor. Those who benefit from the present political and economic structures also live under a false consciousness. They too are dehumanized. They too are in need of liberation. Hence, liberation theology is not a political movement to free the marginalized from oppressive structures; it is a religious movement that strives to bring salvation and liberation to those who fall short of God's will to live abundant and fruitful lives, whether they be the oppressed who are dehumanized or their oppressors who lose their humanity by reaping the rewards from the social structures that privilege them.

Liberation theology is a faith tradition that begins by saying, "¡Basta!"

CHAPTER TWO

Opening the Windows

By the end of the nineteenth century, the United States had moved from an economy of competitive capitalism to one of monopolistic capitalism. With the start of the Spanish-American War (April–August 1898), the United States' quest for economic dominance had begun in earnest. This new stage of capitalism merged with imperialism, finding expression in the spoils of war, specifically in Cuba (as a regent), Puerto Rico (as a colony), and the Philippines (as an imperialist possession). By challenging the declining Spanish Empire, the United States began its first venture in empire building. Rather than acquiring territory (as was the case during Manifest Destiny), the nation began controlling the economies of neighboring nations to obtain financial benefits. This model of economic domination established relationships of dependency even as these territories and countries were nominally independent. The Spanish-American War launched the twentieth century, a period that would be characterized by further economic expansionism. The U.S. military provided the security for U.S. corporations to build roads into developing countries throughout Latin America to extract, by brute force if necessary, their natural resources and cheap labor.

Consider the 1981 interview with Fred Sherwood, former president of the American Chamber of Commerce in Guatemala and the "leading spokesman for the North American business community" in that country. Sherwood arrived in Guatemala in 1954 with the CIA-orchestrated air force that supported the covert overthrow of the democratically elected government of Jacobo Arbenz, Sherwood's investments grew after Arbenz was replaced with a military dictatorship that encouraged the business practices of foreign corporations.

> **Question:** "The State Department says the government hasn't been doing enough to deal with the death squads. Do you think that's reasonable?"
>
> **Sherwood:** "Hell no. Why should we do anything about death squads? They're bumping off the commies, our enemies. I'd give them more power. . . ."
>
> **Question:** "Do all the U.S. businessmen feel the same way?"
>
> **Sherwood:** "Of course they do. After all they're trying to do business. The commies are trying to stop them from doing business . . . to stop the economic growth. . . . It's a hell of violence going around. No one approves of violence, I don't. But if it's a question of them or me, I'd

rather it be them. . . . We grew up on the basis of private enterprise. . . . But these peasants, they don't know how to run something. Really, I'm not downbeating them, but they don't. They're dumb, damn savages."[1]

Without a doubt, a major cause of poverty throughout Latin America has been the foreign and economic policies of the United States and the multinational corporations whose interest the United States protects. Consider the flow of resources during the mid-century. From 1950 to 1955, the United States invested $2 billion in Latin America, mainly in agriculture and new materials. These investments yielded a profit of $3.5 billion, of which almost half returned to the United States.[2]

Resources and raw materials must flow from the periphery toward the center to ensure the supremacy of the world's elite. Because underdevelopment is the flip side of development—that is, the riches of the wealthy are linked to the poverty of the disenfranchised—oppression must be institutionalized in order for the privileged to maintain their position. Hence, a strong military is needed. The U.S. involvement in supporting and maintaining repression throughout Latin America is best illustrated by how we trained and assisted the militaries of various Latin American countries to conduct human rights violations.

The School of the Americas, now known as the Western Hemisphere Institute for Security Cooperation (WHINSEC), located in Fort Benning, Georgia, has trained more than 61,000 Latin American soldiers in commando operations, psychological warfare, and counterinsurgency techniques. The training manuals produced by the Pentagon advocate executions, torture and other forms of physical abuse, false arrest, blackmail, censorship, and payment of bounty for murders. According to former CIA officer John Stockwell, terrorist tactics were, and some would argue still are, central to the U.S. strategy in Central America. He states, "Encouraging techniques of raping women and executing men and children is a coordinated policy of the destabilization program."[3] The CIA's own training manual, *Psychological Operations in Guerrilla Warfare*, developed for the Reagan-administration-sponsored Contra war in Nicaragua, encouraged the assassination of "government officials and sympathizers."[4] Former Rep. Joseph Kennedy (D-Mass.) summarized the significance of the school's U.S.-produced training manuals when he stated, "The Pentagon revealed [through these manuals] what activists opposed to the school have been alleging for years—that foreign military

officers were taught to torture and murder to achieve their political objective."[5]

A congressional task force headed by the late Rep. Joseph Moakley (D-Mass.), concluded that those responsible for many of the government-led massacres in Latin America had been trained by the U.S. Army at Fort Benning, Georgia. These include many from El Salvador; two of the three officers cited for the assassination of Archbishop Oscar Romero in March 1980; three of the four officers cited in the rape and murder of three American nuns and a laywoman in December 1980; Roberto D'Aubuisson, founder of El Salvador's death squads; ten of the twelve officers responsible for the massacre of 900 civilians in El Mozote in December 1981; and nineteen of the twenty-six officers cited in the murder of six Jesuit priests, their housekeeper, and her teenage daughter in November 1989. In addition, brutal military dictators who ruled Bolivia, Argentina, Guatemala, Panama, El Salvador, and Honduras—just to name a few—are all graduates of the school. Probably the most damning indictment of the military school in Fort Benning appeared on its own Web site in 2000: "Many of the [school's] critics supported . . . Liberation Theology . . . in Latin America . . . which was defeated with the assistance of the U.S. Army.[6]

The violence unleashed upon these nations in order to maintain U.S. economic and political supremacy has been justified by calling communists those who rebelled against brutal U.S.-backed dictatorships. In the midst of the Cold War, the simple claim to be fighting communism ensured billions of dollars in military aid and, when needed, military personnel. Brazilian archbishop Dom Hélder Cámara succinctly revealed the hypocrisy of this policy when he famously quipped, "When I give food to the poor, they call me a saint. When I ask why the poor have no food, they call me a communist."[7]

Christian Base Communities

Without those who are oppressed struggling for their liberation, there can be no liberation theology. As important as church conferences and documents have become in creating the religious discourse of liberation theology, they are meaningless if there is no praxis, if those with flesh and blood do not rise up and implement religious views that oppose oppression. Liberation theology is incarnated with the Christian base communities (*comunidades eclesiales de base*—CEBs), which date to the late 1950s. The aims of the CEBs were pastoral, not political, but it was here that the dispossessed gathered to discover how to turn their Christian conviction into a liberative reality within their everyday marginalized lives. Until the establishment of CEBs, many were taught that their poverty was God's will. Now they were learning that their poverty was caused by oppressive

political and economic structures. By 1978, some 150,000 to 200,000 CEBs existed throughout Latin America.[8]

CEBs were small groups of believers who gathered, mainly in the rural areas and the outskirts of urban centers, to worship God and learn from each other how to faithfully live a Christian life that sought to combat the social, political, and economic sins that oppress. They began as a response to the ecclesial reality in which one priest was usually responsible for some 20,000 souls, making it physically impossible for that priest to provide proper counseling and instruction in the faith. Most priests could only concentrate on performing the sacraments during the infrequent times they visited a village or community. The creation of CEBs was a pastoral response to a real need.

At these CEBs, however, the consciousnesses of the oppressed began to be raised. Priests served more as advisors, training the laity in how to lead discussions, usually around a methodology that came to be known as "see-judge-act," a concept we will explore in greater detail in the next chapter. In these small-group discussions, participants began to discover how economic and political structures contributed to their disenfranchisement. In response, they learned how they could implement the liberating message of the Gospels in their lives to bring about salvation—understood as liberation from all sins, communal as well as individual. Theoretically, all theologies are a second act, a reflection of any given community's worldview. But for liberation theology, this second act is the reflection of the actions taken by the poor within these communities.

Secular Revolution

By 1959, the brutal dictatorship of Fulgencio Batista was overthrown by rebels led by Fidel Castro. For the first time, a Catholic Latin American nation fell to what was perceived to be an anti-Catholic communist regime. However, this was not a Marxist-Leninist revolution (even though Fidel Castro's younger brother Raul had ties with Soviet-based movements); rather, the 1959 revolution was first and foremost a third-world rebellion against the subjugation of Cuba to the United States and the passive role played by Christendom. Castro's move toward communism, which occurred after the Bay of Pigs fiasco, had more to do with finding allies to avoid another invasion from the world's strongest superpower than ideological commitments. Regardless of the eventual Marxist commitments or the autocratic rule of Castro, the revolution did serve to demonstrate that nations in Latin American could break free from U.S. hegemony and dependency. While Cuba was not necessarily accepted as a model to emulate by liberationist

thinkers, it did prove that society need not be organized along a pro-U.S. capitalist paradigm.

Inspired by Cuba, rural guerrilla movements sprung up in other Latin American countries, more notably in Venezuela, Bolivia, Guatemala, and Peru. Fearing the possibility of more nations aligning themselves with the Soviet Union, the Kennedy administration launched the Alliance for Progress, a development program modeled on the post–World War II Marshall Plan and tied to strengthening the military in order to combat possible future insurgency threats. The solution for Latin America became an infusion of capital, U.S. know-how, and technology to spur development. The Alliance for Progress was a dismal failure, falling short of most of its own objectives. Hope in reforming economic structures decreased, while suspicion concerning the U.S. model of democratic capitalism increased.

Another consequence of the Cuban Revolution was a 1961 appeal from Pope John XXIII. Aware of the shortage of clergy in Latin America, and fearing that the church might be shut out of another country if it followed Cuba's lead, he invited missionaries to go to Latin America. He asked that North American and European religious orders send 10 percent of their clerics. In response, some priests within the wealthier churches, fearing the advances made by "Marxists," went to serve the poor. Some of these missionaries became radicalized when they encountered the depths of poverty of their new parishioners.

Second Vatican Council

In the 1930s, segments of the Catholic Church in Latin America began moving away from an anti-liberal, anti-science, anti-modernity position and began to wrestle with how to align with progressive socioeconomic movements. They were influenced partially by an official body of papal literature that came to be known as Catholic social teachings, which focused on the church's response to political, economic, and social issues. These writings can be traced to Pope Leo XIII's 1891 encyclical *Rerum Novarum*, which addressed the economic hardships faced by the urban working class throughout Europe. Additionally, in 1931, commemorating the fortieth anniversary of *Rerum Novarum*, Pope Pius XI issued *Quadragesimo Anno*, a strong critique of liberal capitalism.

Encyclicals such as these encouraged the emergence in Latin America of Catholic Action and the specialized groups it promoted: Young Catholic Factory Workers, Young Catholic Farmers, and the Latin American Confederation of Christian Unions. Another important antecedent for Latin American liberation theology occurred in 1955 with the gathering of the general conference of Latin American bishops of the Roman Catholic Church (CELAM I) that met in Rio de Janeiro, Brazil. One of the most important issues explored during the conference was the church's role in missions and in the overall social order. These developments in Latin American Catholicism created great tension and unrest with those in authority, most of which centered on the role clerics should play within society in the face of inhuman conditions caused by political and economic injustice. Hence, when the papacy took up the question of its role in a hurting, modern world, many Latin Americans were ready for the discourse.

The First Vatican Council (1869–1870) mistrusted modernity, science, and democracy. It was more concerned with protecting lands and authority as the Catholic Church's political influence was shrinking. To that end, Vatican I published a *Syllabus of Errors*, which listed eighty views Catholics must reject. Included among the "errors" were freedom to worship, public schools, separation of church and state, and basic democratic principles. The Second Vatican Council (1962–1965) was an attempt by the church to enter the modern world and plot a different course. Elected pope at 77, John XXIII was supposed to be a caretaker due to his advanced age. Influenced by the Catholic social teachings, however, he convened Vatican II to reassess the

role of the church. He liked to say that the purpose of the council was to open the windows to let in "a little fresh air." But what blew through, however, was a tornado!

Vatican II was in session for four years, two months at a time. Although Pope John XXIII died in 1963, his successor, Pope Paul VI, continued the work. Moving away from the hierarchical societal control that had marked its history, the church redefined itself as being on a pilgrimage with the rest of humanity. To that end, the church opened itself more to the world, developing a more accepting attitude. Salvation no longer was to be limited to the Catholic Church. Furthermore, the church was to be understood as the people of God, a community rather than a hierarchy. Most important, the church began moving away from Christendom and its alignment with the powerful. Instead, the church committed itself to be in service to, and in solidarity with, the humble.

Probably the most important document to come out of Vatican II was *Gaudium et Spes*, which called the church to identify with the hopes, joys, griefs, and trials of humanity. The document asserts the independence of the church from political and economic structures while maintaining the responsibility of passing moral judgment on the actions that flow from them. Furthermore, the church recognized its special responsibility for those who are poor or in any way afflicted. Just as influential was the post–Vatican II encyclical *Populorum Progressio* (1967), which focused on international poverty caused by past colonialism as well as newer forms of colonialism. The church now had a responsibility to help bring about structural change. These revolutionary changes in Rome that shifted the church's focus to the poor stimulated, encouraged, emboldened, and justified those who had been for some time moving toward a theology rooted in the Latin American experience. The question they now had to wrestle with was how to contextualize Vatican II in Latin America.

The Revolutionary Priest

In the midst of the Catholic Church's new progressive orientation, Latin American political regimes became more oppressive, as illustrated in the 1964 Brazilian military coup. Brazil probably had the most progressive church in the region, and it was fully engaged in social activism. This came to an end when the military, with U.S. backing, accomplished a *coup d'état*. Many religious leaders disappeared; those who didn't became radicalized. Those who were exiled or who fled took their progressive

liberationist ideas into the new communities in which they found themselves.

Elsewhere, Camilo Torres, a priest and university professor from a wealthy Colombian family, chose a different path in confronting oppression. Finding it difficult to carry out his duties within Christendom, he chose to align himself with the church of the poor. Creating the United Front, he attempted to link workers, peasants (*campesinos*), students, slum dwellers, and trade unionists in a campaign for change. Originally he attempted to work within the system to bring about justice; however, he concluded that reform was unattainable. In response, he turned to revolution. Hanging up his holy vestments in 1965, he took to the hills and joined the Colombian guerrilla revolutionary forces. "I took off my cassock to be more truly a priest," he proclaimed.[9] For Torres, love for the oppressed can at times constrain believers to employ violence. He explained his perspective this way: "I have ceased to say Mass [in order] to practice love for people in temporal, economic and social spheres. . . I think that in this way I follow Christ's injunction, 'Leave thy gifts upon the altar and go first to be reconciled to thy brother.'"[10] In short, action replaces words; praxis replaces theory.

He died in battle in 1966. His radicalization may have inspired other young leftist revolutionaries; however, many within the liberation theological movement considered Torres to have been naive. Even his friend and former classmate Gustavo Gutiérrez did not believe that his decision to join the guerrilla movement was wise.[11] Nevertheless, what Torres added to the discourse was the futility, if not hopelessness, of pursuing reform by working within the system. Torres provided a violent revolutionary alternative.

The Latin American Magna Carta

About 600 bishops from Latin America, along with their advisors, attended the opening session of the Second Vatican Council in 1962. Upon returning home, several of those who either participated in or were influenced by the discussions generated at the council began to wrestle with how the teachings that emerged from the gathering could be implemented within a Latin American context. The church's mandate to help build a new social order resonated among many of them. One such person was Brazilian bishop Dom Hélder Câmara. On August 15, 1967, he organized a group of eighteen bishops from ten nations throughout Latin America, Asia, and Africa to write a letter that moved beyond the recommendations of Pope Paul VI's encyclical *Populorum Progressio*, which had been published five months earlier. The letter proclaimed, "The peoples of the Third World are the proletariats of humanity today. They are exploited by the great nations." What then should

be the response to global injustices? The letter goes on to state, "History shows us that certain revolutions were necessary, and that they have produced good effects." Why revolution? Because the world's wealthy wage "class warfare." "Wealth," the letter concludes, "must be shared by all." The letter's thesis could be summed up as "True socialism is Christianity integrally lived."[12]

Another person with whom a new society resonated was Paulo Freire, a Brazilian educator whose work was influential in providing the intellectual foundation for CEBs—specifically his new methodology for teaching literacy, a process he named *conscientzação*, or consciousness raising. Moving away from a "banking" model of education, which assumed that people were empty vaults in need of deposited knowledge, Freire's Socratic method assumed that people, including the poor, were subjects who brought their own wisdom to the educational process. Moving beyond just teaching

literacy, Freire pioneered a new methodology of popular education that sought the liberation of the oppressed by unmasking the causes of their oppression. Not surprisingly, Freire's concept of *conscientzação* made its way into the influential documents that would later emerge from Medellín.

A more formal attempt to make this new society a reality occurred at a general conference of the Latin American Episcopal Council (CELAM) known as the Medellín Conference, which was held in 1968 in Medellín, Colombia. The theme of the conference was "The Church in the Present Transformation of Latin America in Light of the [Second Vatican] Council." It was attended by 146 bishops and their staff, along with a few nuns, priests, and laypersons. The conference proclaimed that "the Latin American bishops cannot remain indifferent in the face of the tremendous social injustices existent in Latin America, which keep the majority of our people in dismal poverty, which in many cases becomes inhuman wretchedness."[13]

For many, the Medellín Conference is considered the official birthdate of Latin American liberation theology. The task facing those attending the conference was this: How does the church implement the teachings of Vatican II within a Latin American context defined by right-wing military dictatorships and backed by the most powerful nation on earth? What should be the church's response to dictatorships that hold on to power through human rights violations? What is God's response to the suffering of the poor? In reaction to the normalized oppressive existence of the poor in Latin America, the Medellín documents created a theological rejoinder rooted in action. In the next chapter, we will explore this theology in greater detail.

In its attempt to define the church's role, the Medellín Conference produced sixteen documents, of which *Justice,*

Peace, and *Poverty* are considered the most important. These documents boldly proclaimed the role of the church within a Latin American political climate marked by violence, poverty, and death. While both supporters and opponents of liberation theology can find within the Medellín documents passages that strengthen their arguments, as a whole, the documents provided those seeking progressive change with religious justification to struggle for liberation from oppression. More importantly, the conference provided the religious justification for the church to become involved in controversial political programs and movements, thus institutionalizing and legitimizing a radical option for the poor. To that end, the Medellín documents came to be considered the Magna Carta of liberation theology.

The call to praxis can be witnessed in 1971 with the establishment of a political movement begun in Chile, called Christians for Socialism, which called believers to engage in direct political action. Among those who attended the

organizational meeting were eighty priests from throughout Latin America. Although the Medellín documents attempted to remain neutral over which economic course to take, condemning both "liberal capitalism" and "the Marxist system," Christians for Socialism attempted no such impartiality. Its documents clearly stated that there is nothing incompatible between socialism and Christianity. In fact, the mistrust existing between the church and Marxism needed to be remedied. Any preferential option that was made for the poor had to be a socialist option. For many, the salvific economic future of Latin America was based in socialism.[14]

For those U.S.-backed military regimes, this tilt toward socialism not only threatened their hold on power, but it also provided an opportunity to gain additional U.S. military resources to violently put down any threat to their power. By painting those who questioned the injustices of the regime as Marxists taking orders from the Soviet Union via communist Cuba, a free hand was given to suppress and even eliminate dissention. Maintaining economic and political oppression that benefited the commercial interests of U.S. businesses was characterized as "our" fight against communists to prevent "another Cuba."

Liberation

By 1971, those participating in the economic development conversations that arose from the Medellín Conference began to move away from the concept of development, choosing the more proactive word *liberation*. In May of that year, Hugo Assmann conducted a symposium in Montevideo, Uruguay, titled, "Oppression-Liberation: The Challenge to Christians." That same year, Leonardo Boff published in Brazil a series of articles under the title *Jesus Christ Liberator*. The series was translated into English seven years later. Probably one of the most important publications, which became the definitive description of liberation theology, was Gustavo Gutiérrez's *A Theology of Liberation* (1971; English translation in 1973). The book was a reflection on how theology could be constructed by learning from the daily struggles of the poor, and it became the primary text by which many came to learn about liberation theology. The genesis of Gutiérrez's book occurred in 1969 while Gutiérrez was on a transatlantic flight for a conference on the church's role in socioeconomic development. While reviewing his notes on the paper he was planning to give, "The Meaning of Development," Gutiérrez wondered why he was using the term *development* when what was really needed was liberation. Hence, he crossed out his title and renamed the paper, "Notes on Theology of Liberation."[15]

CHAPTER THREE

Liberation Theologies: What Are They?

During an August 29, 2010, interview on Fox News Sunday, the day after his quasi-religious rally on the steps of the Lincoln Memorial in Washington, DC, Glenn Beck backpedaled from his earlier accusations that President Obama was a racist with "deep-seated hatred for white people or the white culture." During his interview with Chris Wallace, Beck said, "I didn't understand, really, [Obama's] theology. . . . I think that it is much more of a theological question that he is a guy who understands the world through liberation theology, which is oppressor and victim." Beck described liberation theology "as a direct opposite of what the gospel is talking about" and "Marxism disguised as religion." In a comment made on July 13, 2010, during his popular television program, Beck labeled liberation theology as having "completely perverted Christianity and teaching something radically different. For example, [black liberationist theologian James] Cone himself has argued that the Bible is insufficient to know what social justice is and that you need Marxism to understand what Christianity means."

Beck went so far as to warn his listeners during another one of his shows (March 2, 2010) that if their priests, pastors, or ministers use the phrase *social justice* on Sundays, they should leave that church. He begged his listeners, "Look for the words *social justice* or *economic justice* on your church Web site. If you find it, run as fast as you can. Social justice and economic justice—they are code words. Now, am I advising people to leave their church? Yes!"

Beck is not the only person who has demonized liberation theology (although he does hold a particularly limited and erroneous understanding of it). Like Beck, some simplistically have dismissed liberation theology as Marxism in religious garb, or as a passing fad dated from the 1960s through the 1980s. Yet liberation theology in its many manifestations continues to influence the thoughts and spirituality of the world's wretched. For this reason, we now turn our attention to some of the basic theological and theoretical themes of liberation theology.

Message

The message of liberation theology can be reduced to the purpose of Jesus Christ's ministry as articulated in the Gospel of John: "I have come that they might have life and have it more abundantly" (10:10). To experience life more abundantly is not limited to waiting for some eschatological future; the message of Christ is for the here and now. This abundant life that Jesus claims to offer reveals that God is a God of life, not a God of death. <u>Structures or individuals that bring death are anti-Christ.</u> Hence, the gospel message of liberation that is found in Christ stresses liberation from all forms of human oppression, be they social, economic, political, racial, sexual, environmental, or religious. Liberation theology becomes the process of integrating faith with the sociopolitical everyday in which the oppressed find themselves.

In a very real sense, liberation is salvation. The Hebrew word *yāša'*, and the Greek term *sōzō* appear in most English translations of the Bible as "save," yet they also mean

"liberate." Salvation is neither an abstract concept nor a personal feeling; rather, it is a state of being that encompasses rescue and deliverance. Hence the question: Salvation/liberation from what? From what are we rescued and delivered? To be liberated from sin, personal or corporate, is to be saved. Among liberationists, both words (*liberation* and *salvation*) are used interchangeably.

The goal of salvation, of liberation, is to break with sin through a new life in Christ. Salvation is achieved through the process of consciousness raising, learning how structures of oppression prevent believers from experiencing the abundant life promised by Christ. Thus, the evangelical goal of liberation theology is not to convince nonbelievers to believe doctrinal tenets; it is to convince nonpersons of their personhood because they, regardless of what the world tells them, are created in the very image of God. In this fashion, the purpose of theology is not to create, expand, or sustain doctrinal beliefs; rather, it is to respond to the inhuman conditions in which the vast majority of humanity lives. In a very real sense, theologies of liberation are a collection of religious reflections that provide theological grounding for actions that can lead to the rescue and deliverance of all who face sociocultural and economic oppression. It is a call for both personal and collective transformation.

Contextual

There is not a single liberation theology upon which everyone agrees; there are many liberation theologies. The reason for this is that all theology is contextual (including Eurocentric theologies); all theology is rooted in the social location of those seeking faith-based responses to their situation. Whatever liberation looks like, it can only be determined by the people living under oppressive structures. How rural

Colombians understand God's response to their condition is different from how Asian-Americans in New York City understand God's movements. Different ethnicities, geographical locations, and oppressive structures lead to different understandings about theology, even though congruency can be found around the message of Christ's gift of abundant life. Any attempt to provide a unified definition of liberation theology is therefore problematic, even though the theology expresses a conceptualized faith's response to the reality faced by the dispossessed and disenfranchised.

Although the common starting point of theological reflection is the existential experience of the marginalized, the ultimate goal remains liberation from the reality of societal misery. Not all who are disenfranchised have a similar

experience; thus, all theologies are indigenous, unable to be exported into a different social location as if they were some sort of commodity. How African-Americans in the urban centers do liberation theology will differ from how undocumented Mexican-Americans on the southern border understand God. And while the focus thus far has been on a Christian-based liberation theology, we will see later that there are liberative theologies from the perspectives of different faith and spiritual traditions.

Pastoral

Liberation theology is oriented toward the future: What can I do to bring about God's salvation? How can the disenfranchised be enabled to discover the path toward their salvation and liberation? Most liberationists are more than simply academicians; they are pastoral agents, working with and for the disenfranchised. Their concern has less to do with developing a scholarly body of religious thought called liberation theology and more to do with standing in solidarity with faith-based grassroots movements whose ultimate goal is social justice. Consequently, liberation theology is more concerned with engaging in an open dialogue with the world, rather than preserving the status quo.

Latin American moral theologian Francisco Moreno Rejón observed that a salient note in liberation theology is rooted in the effort to reconcile the requirements of a theoretical, academic order with a pastoral concern. Far from repeating timeless ahistorical principles, liberation theology presents itself as a reflection vigorously involved with the people's daily experience. For liberationists, all praxis chosen is derived from the perspective of the oppressed. From the underside of power and privilege, a worldview is developed from which to address existing structural injustices.

Methodology

Eurocentric theological thought is normatively done deductively: from theory (or truth) comes action (or praxis). First comes some conceptualized universal truth, such as the Bible or church teachings. Based on this truth, an action is determined and implemented. Thus, orthopraxis (correct action) flows from orthodoxy (correct doctrine). The liberationist turns this methodology on its head by arguing that theology is the second step, as orthodoxy instead flows from orthopraxis. Beyond the historical experiences and the social locations where individuals act as social agents, truth cannot be ascertained. Only through justice-based praxis, engaged in transforming society, can individuals come closer to understanding God's will. From understanding the social location in which the oppressed find themselves, through the praxis of consciousness raising

to understand the causes of oppression, comes a theological response. In the doing of liberative acts, theory (theology) is formed as a reflection of praxis.

Liberation theology is thus a praxis-centered theology which recognizes that before we can do theology, we must do liberation while connecting the spiritual with material realities. Those implementing liberation theology as a spiritual response to material disenfranchisement follow a "see-judge-act" paradigm (borrowed from the Young Christian Workers of the 1930s), recognizing that we must first do liberative praxis before we can do liberation theology. Simply stated, believers *see* the oppression that is occurring. Through the act of consciousness raising, they *judge* the causes of oppression. Finally they commit themselves to *act*. The praxis implemented is informed by considerations of social analysis, philosophy, and biblical hermeneutics. This

action is a reflective praxis rooted in the experience of the oppressed. Such praxis brings us back to *see*, where the impact of action is evaluated.

Faith is manifested in what is done to "the least of these"—the hungry, the thirsty, the naked. As the Letter of James reminds us, "Faith without works is dead" (2:26). Only through praxis do we get to see the face of God. This is a religious perspective that does the gospel rather than simply meditates on it. Still, the popular movements for liberation should not be confused with liberation theology. Liberation theology is forged in the reflection of social actions taken so as to humanize inhuman conditions. Theological reflection concerning social activism, in other words—where or who God is in the midst of oppression—is what becomes liberation theology.

God of the Oppressed

Liberation theology begins with the poor, the oppressed, the marginalized, the outcast, and the disenfranchised. To do liberation theology is to do it with and from the perspective of those whom society considers as nobodies. Incarnating theological thought among those who are dispossessed roots liberation theology in the material as opposed to simply the metaphysical. Within the Eurocentric context, the primary religious question concerns the existence of God. Among most liberationists, the struggle is not with God's existence per se, but with God's character. Who is this God whom we say exists? What is the character of God?

Whoever God is, God imparts and sustains life while opposing death. Wherever lives are threatened with poverty and oppression, God is *presente*—present. The God of the Gospels is offended by the dehumanizing conditions in which the marginalized find themselves. This is a God who acts in history, a God who hears the cries of the enslaved Hebrews, physically enters history, and leads God's people to the promised land. It is in the everyday where one can encounter God. But while God is present in history, constructing a new society remains a human project. God may lead God's people to a promised land, but the people must commit to the praxis of walking there.

To enter history and stand in solidarity with the oppressed means that God takes sides over and against the rich and powerful, not because the marginalized are better Christians or holier people, but because they are oppressed. In short, God makes a preferential option for the poor and oppressed. This is the God whom the Hebrews called *Go'el*, the one who provides justice for the weak, makes a home for the alien, becomes a parent to the orphan, and comforts

the widow—biblical euphemisms for the most vulnerable within society. The type of worship that best honors this God is the doing of justice (Isa. 1:10–17).

Through Jesus, this God knows what it means to suffer under religious and politically unjust structures. Because Jesus—in the ultimate act of solidarity with all who continue to be persecuted today—carries the wounds upon his feet, hands, and side, God knows what it means to exist in solidarity with all who are being crucified on the crosses of sexism, racism, ethnic discrimination, classism, and heterosexism. Those who suffer under oppression have a God who understands their suffering. Because Jesus suffered oppression on the cross, a divine commitment to stand against injustices exists, a stance believers are called to emulate. In short, to know God is to do justice. To stand by while oppression occurs is to profess nonbelief, regardless of any confession given privately or publicly.

Jesus Christ Liberator

Christ does not reside in some heavenly abode; rather, he dwells among us. Jesus, as God in flesh, chose poverty. The miracle of the incarnation is not that God became human, but that God became poor. For Christians, faith turns on the life, death, and resurrection of Jesus, who becomes a model to imitate through liberative praxis. While Eurocentric theologians normatively focus on Jesus' death as redemptive and salvific, many liberationist thinkers view Jesus' entire existence, from birth to resurrection, as liberative. The cross is meaningless except for fidelity to Christ's mission. For many, the crucifixion has less to do with an act of atonement than an act of solidarity. Jesus' condemnation to death is the ultimate consequence faced by many who struggle for justice. He takes up his cross as the definitive act of solidarity with all who are called the crucified people, those who continue to be crucified today.

One of the phrases often repeated by Jesus is that the reign of God is at hand. For Jesus, God's reign was not some future event, but a reality that can be experienced here and now. Historically, the reward of some hereafter has been used to encourage submission to oppression as an earthly trial in preparation for heavenly riches. But the proclamation that God's reign is at hand signaled that salvation is for now, not for some by and by. All too often, Christ's crucifixion is spiritualized, despite the fact that that moment in history was a political as well as a religious act. Crucifixion recognizes that death-dealing actions are the usual response from the authorities who protect the power and privilege of the few. Regardless of the possible consequences, however, those who claim to be disciples of Jesus

stand against injustices because Christ's life illustrated that the heart of God's reign is justice. To follow Jesus is to seek liberation from all forms of oppression. Such a lifestyle fulfills the greatest commandments: to love God and to love one's neighbor as oneself.

To become a Christian is to become a new creature in Christ. This transformation includes liberation from exploitation so that humans can live a more humane and dignified life through the abolition of injustice. To seek liberation is to strive toward a new society, the establishment of God's reign on earth. Contrary to Glenn Beck's protestations, if a tree is known by its fruit, then social justice becomes the fruit by which Christianity is recognized. The resurrection signifies a decisive triumph over not only death but also oppression. It brings new life and vindicates Jesus' liberative message.

The Good Book

For many Christian liberationists, the biblical text holds an authoritative place, although not a fundamentalist or literal place. It is a book of life, not a collection of ancient stories, that becomes authoritative when read through one's own eyes and interpreted to fit the present situation. This means that the biblical text is understood contextually, through the experiences of the oppressed who, in turn, reinterpret their social location through biblical symbols. For the liberationists, not only has God spoken, but God continues to speak, and God has something important to say about the oppression of the poor. Biblical narratives become means by which to hear God speak throughout history and to perceive where we stand in relationship to this God.

For example, the creation stories at the beginning of Genesis reveal a cosmos that is good and a God whose will is for humanity to live in harmony with the earth and the one who created all that is. "God saw everything that God had made, and behold, it was very good" (Gen. 1:31). The book of Exodus becomes a prototype for liberation. An enslaved people look toward God for their liberation. This is a God who enters into their reality and leads them toward a promised land. This God tells Moses, "I have seen the affliction of my people . . . and have heard their cry. . . . I know their sorrow and have come down to deliver them" (Exod. 3:7–8). The message of all the prophets can be summarized in one word: *justice*. The prophets rail against God's people whenever they fail "to search justice; help the oppressed; be just to the orphan, and strive for the widow" (Isa. 1:17).

Sin

According to Leonardo Boff, what social analysis calls "structural poverty," faith calls "structural sin," and what social analysis calls "the private accumulation of wealth," faith calls "the sin of selfishness." Suffering exists because sin represents the root of all that is wrong with the world. Sin is responsible for the enslavement of humanity; it forces individuals to act against their best interest. Sin can be the outcome of individuals' choices, or it can be the ramifications of the prevailing social structures.

For liberationists, sin is communal. All sins, even those committed by individuals, have communal ramifications. All too often, Eurocentric theology has made sin and its redemption personal. Sin becomes an act of commission or omission, while salvation from our sinfulness rests in a *personal* savior in the form of Jesus Christ. Conversion, however, is never personal but must extend to social transformation. What is missing from Eurocentric religious thought is the structural nature of sin. Oppression and

poverty as expressions of sin are mostly caused by societal structures that are designed to enrich the few at the expense of the many.

God's will is for all to share the fruits of the earth. Contrary to God's will is what has come to be known as the dependency theory, which maintains that the world's industrial nations (the United States, Europe, the former Soviet Union, and Japan) of the North have grown prosperous at the expense of the global South (Latin America, Africa, and parts of Asia). Because the consequences of these socioeconomic structures cause death, they are understood to be sinful. A person with a gun can murder a child. We have no difficulty in characterizing such a heinous violent act as sin.

But death does not solely come from the barrel of a gun. Death is also caused by economic, social, and political structures. While all may feel horror at the brutal and violent death of a child, most fail to notice the roughly 30,000 children who die of hunger and preventable diseases every day.[1]

Yet while these children are perishing, impoverished countries are spending three to five times more on paying off foreign debt than providing basic services that can alleviate this silent genocide. We are quick to label the brutal shooting of a single child a sin, while we ignore the 30,000 children who die slowly over a period of years. Liberationists see that the deaths of these thousands of children, caused by a global economic structure (neoliberalism) that is designed to benefit those located in the so-called first

world is as much a sin as violently shooting children. This form of sin has come to be known as institutional violence.

The ultimate aim is to go beyond reform, for reform attempts to make sinful societal structures more bearable while maintaining capital in the hands of the few. Liberationists envision a new creation free of injustices, where human dignity and the freedom to seek one's own destiny reign supreme. Liberationists call for social revolution, a radical change of the structures that cause oppression, a move closer to Jesus' explanation of why he came: to provide an abundant life.

The Church

Liberation theology recognizes that Christendom has been closely linked to the dominant culture and to the political structures designed to protect the interests of the privileged few. By contrast, liberationists focus on human needs rather than ecclesiastical dogma. They believe that the church can never be neutral in the face of injustices. When the church stands in solidarity with the marginalized, it ceases to be an extension of Christendom and instead becomes the church of the oppressed. In this way, the church fulfills the mission of Christ who said, "The Spirit of the Lord is upon me, and anointed me to preach the good news to the poor, to heal the brokenhearted, to bring freedom to the enslaved, to provide sight to those who cannot see, to proclaim liberation to the oppressed, and to announce the acceptable year of the Lord" (Luke 4:18–19).

For the liberationists, God is never found in lavish cathedrals, whose ornate steeples serve as monuments to those who reached the pinnacle of wealth on the backs of the poor and disenfranchised. God is only found in the

gathering of the "least of these," the same place Jesus resided during his earthly ministry. We are called to follow Jesus in struggling with and for the oppressed, as well as in learning about God from the oppressed. Crucial to the liberationist process is breaking the tie between the privileged powerful and Christendom so that the church, the coming together of believers, can occur. Latin American liberationists argue that the church must live in solidarity with the poor, incarnated among the oppressed. Its mission is to serve the world as a witness to God's will for life.

The church not only evangelizes the oppressed, but it is in turn evangelized by the oppressed. Hence, the church is called not only to signify liberation, but also to be an instrument by which liberation is achieved. Although liberation theologians are scholars, they attempt to root their academics within the faith community. This understanding of church separates liberation theologians from most academicians. Liberationist scholars work as "organic intellectuals" à la Antonio Gramsci, connecting the intellectual enterprise with popular movements. Their scholarly contributions also raise the consciousness of those who are unaware of their complicity with oppressive power structures, and of those who may be aware and who already are committed to working in and with disenfranchised communities during their struggle for salvation/liberation. These liberationist academicians operate as scholar-activists who theorize and theologize for the express purpose of changing oppressive social structures, as opposed simply to understanding better said structures for the sake of scholarship alone.

Marxist?

A major critique of liberation theology has been its supposed link with Marxism. Commitment to liberation for a Christian does not necessarily mean a commitment to some political revolutionary ideology; rather, it first and foremost refers to the place where God is encountered. Liberation is a prayerful and spiritual encounter with God that leads us beyond the self toward serving the other, and then leads us back to prayer. While it is true that most (if not all) liberation theologians express opposition to capitalism and multinational corporations, it is also true that a few liberation theologians have considered themselves to be Marxist, believing that Marx and the Bible coincide in their aim of bringing about justice. Nevertheless, even these liberation theologians have consistently argued that their commitment has always been for liberation, not Marx.

Although liberation theology's roots of encountering the oppressed with God are mystical, they can never be reduced to the spiritual. Unlike the Eurocentric norm, there exists no dichotomy in liberation theology between sacred and secular space. Hence, to be faithful to God spills over to the everyday, engaging economic, political, and cultural matters. For many, the causes of oppression are economically based; therefore, an alternative socioeconomic system is needed—a structure that moves away from what Pope John Paul II called "savage" capitalism. Liberationists insist on employing whatever social-scientific methodologies can best elucidate the causes of oppression. Not surprisingly, several have found Marxist economic theories helpful in explaining the plight of the poor.

Marxist economic analysis can be used as a tool for dreaming up new realities, but using it in this way does not equal embracing a comprehensive Marxist worldview. Leonardo Boff probably says it best: "Marx and his comrades interest us to the degree that they help us better understand the reality of exploitation and point to possible ways of overcoming the capitalist system, which is harmful to the people and excludes them from participation."[2] Most liberationists would reject the negative view of religion, the autonomy of the economic superstructure, and the identification of the poor with the wider category "proletariat" that one finds in Marxism. Others would critique the bureaucratism and militant atheism characteristic of the Soviet Union and other countries that rooted themselves in Marxism. One would be hard-pressed to find any liberationists who advocate adopting a Cuba-style social order. In fact, during the Medellín Conference, many saw themselves caught between capitalism and Marxism. For liberationists, Marxist analysis can be employed without accepting its philosophical materialism or atheism. The point of departure for justice-based praxis is

faith, and anything outside of the realm of faith, including Marxism, falls short.

Marx may be one of many conversation partners, but he can never be the sole guide into the future. Even though little can be found in the works of liberationists that directly engages Marxism, these scholars understand and at times use Marxist theory, specifically the concept of class struggle. Most liberationists accept class struggle as a reality experienced by the oppressed, even though they do not advocate for it. To understand the causes of poverty and oppression by using Marxist analysis does not mean that liberationists embrace a Marxist worldview.

Unlike most Americans, liberationists distinguish between Marxism and socialism, and many of them advocate some socialist form of organization, such as the Christian base communities discussed in the previous chapter. Unfortunately, any use of Marx within an anti-Marxist U.S. milieu usually ends any objective conversation; most Americans equate Marxism with Leninist-Stalinist totalitarian regimes.

This sentiment was exploited by Latin American right-wing military dictatorships during the 1970s and '80s who discovered that if they could characterize liberation theology as a Marxist movement akin to the Cuban Revolution, then the United States would provide military resources for wiping out any threat to the status quo, regardless of how abusive or repressive the existing government was. Hence, popular movements against political repression were suppressed by labeling them Marxist, even though those protesting government abuses were probably more influenced by the Gospel of Mark than they were the Gospel of Marx.

CHAPTER FOUR

Early Proponents

On March 24, 1980, a single shot rang out in a small hospital chapel in El Salvador. The archbishop celebrating the Mass was shot in the chest. The archbishop's assassination occurred because he dared to stand in solidarity with the poor and to raise the consciousness of those suffering under political and economic oppression. Originally an opponent of liberation theology, Oscar A. Romero was converted early in his tenure as archbishop shortly after his friend and fellow priest Rutilio Grande was assassinated by the government. In the three years Romero served as archbishop, he became known as "the voice of the voiceless." A month before he was killed, Romero said this during an interview:

> My life has been threatened many times. I have to confess that, as a Christian, I don't believe in death without resurrection. If they kill me, *I will rise again in the Salvadoran people.* . . . If God accepts the sacrifice of my life, my hope is that my blood will be like a seed of liberty and a sign that our hopes will soon become a reality. My death will be for the liberation of my people and a testimony of hope for a future. A bishop will die, but the church of God, which is the people, will never perish.[1]

Oscar Romero is but one of the 75,000 (conservatively estimated) who were killed during El Salvador's civil war, most of whom were civilians. Although no official numbers exist, hundreds of thousands of the "very least of these" throughout Latin America died or disappeared during the 1960s, '70s, and '80s. These deaths were committed or sanctioned by right-wing military regimes financed and encouraged by the U.S. government.

In the midst of this carnage, church leaders and thinkers risked their lives to articulate a theological perspective rooted in the everyday experience of those being slaughtered. Unlike most theologies created from the safety of armchairs located in prestigious universities, liberation theology was forged where the blood of martyrs was routinely spilled. Willingness to stand in solidarity with the many being crucified decisively shaped the early discourse of liberation theology. Many of these early proponents' names were also on the military's death lists. Others were threatened, tortured, persecuted, and/or exiled. Their own social location influenced how they came to articulate a different way of perceiving the face of the Divine.

This chapter will briefly examine a few of the early liberationist thinkers and their major contributions. Obviously, not everyone can be included in such limited space, nor can

the thoughts of those mentioned be explored in depth. Nevertheless, this chapter will identify some of the most salient contributors to the discourse.

Gustavo Gutiérrez

A Peruvian priest of Indian ancestry, Gustavo Gutiérrez (b. 1928), is probably the best known and most influential liberation theologian, having drafted many of the movement's early primary documents. His groundbreaking 1971 book, translated into English in 1973 as *A Theology of Liberation*, was among the first definitive elucidations of the theology. Gutiérrez's works attempt to provide a pastoral answer to the question of how Christians can live a life that is faithful to God and neighbor as manifested among the poor. He reflects on possible answers from the perspective of his ministry in the Rimac slum of Lima. There he

65

discovers that God is found through one's neighbor. Specifically, he proclaims, "To know God is to do justice, is to be in solidarity with the poor person."[2]

In the midst of trials and tribulations, Gutiérrez seeks a new way to do theology in order to make Christianity relevant and liberative at the underside of history. Theology ceases to be doctrinal truths created by the intelligentsia for the common people to believe; instead, it becomes a reflection of actions taken to end human suffering—a critical reflection based on praxis in light of God's word, especially the exodus narrative and the incarnation of Christ. This critical response is a people's theology that begins and is formulated at the grassroots among the poor who are seeking and confronting the injustices under which they are forced to exist. Its purpose is that they, the poor, can become agents of their own history. Their acts of and for justice produce theology. The goal of theology is no longer just to understand the world, but to change it; it is, in effect, to liberate suffering humanity, the church, and society from idolatry, ideology, and alienation.

For Gutiérrez, liberation has three meanings. The first refers to the aspirations of the poor, encompassing their liberation from sin, specifically societal sin in the form of social, political, and economic structures that cause oppression. The second meaning refers to the ability of individuals (and Latin American nations) to determine their own destiny. Finally, liberation refers to the freedom found in Christ.

Leonardo Boff

Leonardo Boff (b. 1938), probably the most prolific among the Latin American liberationists, is a former Franciscan priest who taught theology at the Franciscan Theological Institute in Petrópolis, Brazil. For him, the purpose of liberation theology is to echo and respond to the challenges that the church faces, always accenting the communal. His emphasis on praxis leads him to conclude, "It is not those who are Christians who are good, true, and just. Rather, the good, the true, and the just are Christians."[3]

Boff's major contribution to the liberationist discourse has been his work in creating a Christology "from below," as evident in his 1972 groundbreaking book, translated in 1978 as *Jesus Christ Liberator*. Boff attempts to understand who Christ is today by focusing on the actions and teachings of the Jesus of history. For him, Jesus is foremost a liberator from the human condition, seeking liberation (nonviolently) from economic, social, and political structures. This is a Christ who is more concerned with the needs of the suffering masses than church dogma, a Christ indigenous to the Latin American experience of whom we ask: What can Christ do for the oppressed?

Consequently, this is a Christ who is rooted in the everyday, in open dialogue with the world, in seeking liberation for the voiceless from the structural evils that transcend individual evils, and in emphasizing liberation-in-act over liberation-in-thought. Boff gives prominence to Jesus' central teachings concerning the kingdom of God, a kingdom that, because it is somewhat realized within history, is significant for the concept of human liberation and freedom. According to Boff, "Christ understands himself as Liberator because he preaches, presides over, and is already inaugurating the kingdom of God."[4]

His book *Church: Charism and Power* attempted to deemphasize the institutional church's power structures. Boff argued that since the fourth century, the church has traded the power that comes from the gospel for a monarchical hierarchy. His writings elicited a formal Vatican inquiry that eventually led to his silencing; hence, Boff was

unable to speak publicly or to write. His silencing led to his eventually leaving the priesthood.

Clodovis Boff

Clodovis Boff (b. 1944) is a Servite priest and the brother of Leonardo Boff, with whom he has coauthored several books. For years, Clodovis Boff would spend six months a year doing pastoral work in the Amazon jungle among the rubber gatherers, whose way of life was gradually disappearing. Walking miles with an infected foot through the roadless region of Acre in western Brazil and sharing in the lives, work, and struggles of the people to whom he ministered, Boff would reflect on his day-to-day experiences at the grassroots to formulate what he called a "feet-on-the-ground" theology. This is a theology first worked out with one's feet; it is rooted in the physical space shared by the marginalized. The grueling walk took hours, leaving Boff with the bruised feet necesssary to better appreciate the plight of the poor. The other half of the year he would teach and write at the university on this methodology of joining praxis with academics.

Along with six other priests, Boff was removed from his teaching position from Pontifical Catholic University in 1984 for his views on liberation theology. Ironically, in the fall of 2008, he wrote an article for the journal *Revista Ecle- siástica Brasileira*, for which his brother Leonardo used to be editor until he was silenced by the Vatican, denouncing liberation theology. In the article, Clodovis breaks with the foundational principle of liberation theology, which he describes as the error of making the poor the first operative principle of theology, replacing God and Jesus with them. He calls for a return to the original foundation of Christ. Clodovis's article brought a forceful rebuke from his brother Leonardo, who characterized Clodovis's thinking as wrong, theoretically erroneous, and pastorally harmful.

Juan Luis Segundo

Juan Luis Segundo (1925–1996) was a Jesuit priest born in Uruguay. A prolific author, he is considered one of the main architects of liberation theology. In 1965, he cofounded the Centro de Investigación y Acción Social Pedro Fabro (Peter Faber Center of Theological and Social Studies) in Montevideo, Uruguay, to investigate the relationship between religion and society. Segundo's criticism of the government led to the center's closure in 1971. Prior to Vatican II, Segundo was publishing on the themes that would eventually become liberation theology, specifically the importance of Latin America's forging its theological perspectives apart from Europe. He saw theology as a reflection of the experiences of ordinary believers, not an academic discipline that can claim neutrality while masking an ideology that protects the interests of the dominant culture. For Segundo, the church must acknowledge that it does not have all the answers and instead accomplish its mission of serving the people through revolutionary praxis committed to transforming the reality of the oppressed.

Segundo was the most prominent thinker in the development of the liberationist methodology known as the hermeneutical circle, which interprets the word of God in light of the present situation faced by the oppressed. From liberating praxis, a theology is constructed that informs a newer liberating praxis. Segundo rejected "the naive belief that the word of God is applied to human realities inside some antiseptic laboratory that is totally immune to the ideological tendencies and struggles of the present day. . . . Each new

reality obliges us to interpret the word of God afresh, to change reality accordingly, and then to go back and reinterpret the word of God again."[5] As reality changes, so too do the questions we have for God, forcing the standard and dogmatic interpretations of God's word to change.

The first step of the hermeneutical circle recognizes that how we experience reality leads to ideological suspicion. In the second step, our ideological suspicion is applied to the entire ideological superstructure, specifically in its attempt to "deideologize" theology. In the third step, experiencing reality leads us to be suspicious of the prevailing biblical interpretations for not taking enough of the present reality into account. The circle ends with a new hermeneutic, a way of interpreting the biblical text with the new information we possess. Consequently, God's word will always have something important to say about the present reality faced by humanity.

Jon Sobrino

A Jesuit theologian born in Spain to a Basque family, Jon Sobrino (b. 1938) has spent over fifty years teaching and ministering in the midst of the violence in El Salvador. He survived an assassination attempt on November 16, 1989, when members of the U.S.-trained Salvadoran military broke into the rectory and murdered six fellow Jesuits. His work focuses on Christology and its link to spirituality. Like Leonardo Boff, Sobrino emphasizes the close parallels between Jesus' social location and the contemporary context in which Latin Americans find themselves; Christology, therefore, needs to be done from the "underside of history," which means beginning with the actual events that occurred in the life of Jesus and that continue to occur in the lives of the oppressed.

For Sobrino, who draws on Ellacuría's work, the oppressed are crucified today, just as surely as Jesus was crucified some two thousand years ago at Golgotha. The poor and oppressed are the crucified people of today; like Jesus, they provide an essential soteriological perspective on our history. Sobrino insists that God chooses those who are oppressed in history—the hungry, the thirsty, the naked, the alien, the sick, the prisoner—and makes them the principal means of salvation, just as God chose the "suffering servant," the crucified Christ, to bring salvation to the world. Because there can be no salvation apart from the poor, the church must find its purpose and unity in serving the poor.

The God who suffers does not appear to the Pharaohs or Caesars of history, those responsible for this suffering.

Leaders of empires, then and now, whose policies cause death to God's people are more aligned with the satanic than with the divine. For this reason, God appears to their slaves, their vassals, and those disenfranchised by the empire.

In 2007, the Vatican's Congregation for the Doctrine of the Faith admonished Sobrino. A notification was issued declaring his writings to be erroneous and dangerous, and as such, potentially harmful to the faithful.

Ignacio Ellacuría

Ignacio Ellacuría (1930–1989) was born in Spain and worked as a Jesuit priest in El Salvador. As rector of Central American University (UCA), he taught alongside fellow professor Jon Sobrino. His work focused on the philosophical foundation of liberation theology. Along with Jon Sobrino, he coedited *Mysterium Liberationis: Fundamental Concepts of Liberation Theology*, the definitive systematic summary of liberation theology written by many of the leading Latin American thinkers of the movement. At one o'clock in the morning on November 16, 1989, he was roused from his bed at the rectory in UCA and, along with four fellow Jesuits, was dragged to the garden at gunpoint and shot in the head. Elsewhere on the premises, the soldiers found the priests' cook, Julia Elba Ramos, her fifteen-year-old daughter, and a seventy-year-old priest; they murdered these three as well. Before leaving, the soldiers painted pro-guerrilla slogans and staged a fake firefight to blame the anti-government forces of the FMLN. Their deaths were a turning point in the Salvadoran civil war and helped spread Ellacuría's work beyond a Latin American audience.

Enrique Dussel

A theologian, historian, priest, prolific author, and a primary founder of the theme "philosophy of liberation," Enrique Dussel (b. 1934) was born in Argentina. In October 1973, he escaped an assassination attempt by a paramilitary group who firebombed his house. By 1975, he was placed second on the military's death list, which forced him into exile in Mexico. As a scholar, he understands the global order to be divided between the ruling elites from the center (North America, Europe, and the then Soviet Union) and those residing at the periphery, specifically Latin America, Africa, and parts of Asia. Dussel analyzes the alienation of these peripheral people caused by over five centuries of colonialism and imperialism.

The universal truths and knowledge expounded by the ruling elites, who define themselves as the missionaries of

civilization, undergird what has come to be defined as human nature. Those who stand up against the center, in effect, stand up against nature, God, and God's will. Those not in the center are characterized as nonbeings in need of the center's paternal, civilizing hand. Power, domination, and the center become identical. What has come to be known as Western philosophy, in effect, legitimizes the global economic, political, and social domination of people on the periphery. Consequently, any true hope for a just future must rest with the liberation of the periphery people through subverting the established unjust order.

José Porfirio Miranda

José Porfirio Miranda (1924–2001) was a Mexican Marxist philosopher, an economist, an ex-Jesuit, and a biblical scholar who served as an advisor to worker and student groups throughout Mexico. Disconnected from the church and theological colleagues, he is among the few who advocated linking the biblical faith with Marxism, the apostle Paul with Marx. In his work, love and justice are inseparable concepts that take on meaning within a social context. The only way to know and love God is to love one's neighbor as manifested in doing justice for, with, and toward one's neighbor. Miranda points out that in the first Christian community, members sold their possessions and held everything in common so that each could have according to his needs (Acts 2:44–45). To enter God's kingdom, one first had to renounce private property (Mark 10:21, 25); thus, only the poor could enter (Luke 6:20). No one is able to serve both God and money (Matt. 6:24). Thus, all must choose between capitalism and this world, or communism and God; there is no third way. Ironically, in a 1985 essay titled "Is Marxism Essentially Atheistic?" Miranda rejected Marxism, concluding that it is based on a false reductionism.

José Miguez Bonino

Born in Argentina, José Miguez Bonino (1924–2012) was a Methodist minister and was considered one of the leading Protestant liberationists. Although most of the better-known Latin American theologians were and are Catholics, several Protestants have also contributed to the formation and development of the theology, among them Bonino, who served as president of the World Council of Churches. He stressed that liberationists are not socialist or Marxist ideologues, but rather "a new breed of Christians" committed to form a new society comprised of liberated humans. Thus, their social activism is the result of their faith.

Years before liberation theology, a group of Protestants, including Bonino and led by Richard Shaull, formed in 1961 an organization called Iglesia y Sociedad en América Latina (ISAL; in English, Churches and Society in Latin America). ISAL advocated a "theology of revolution" that promoted socialist revolutions, although not necessarily violent ones. Believing that modest reform was inadequate, ISAL's theology of revolution was an attempt to move Protestants out of their pietistic tradition and into a transformative social activism with and for the oppressed. By the late 1960s, ISAL had moved away from the language of revolution and toward the language of liberation. The works of Bonino and other Protestants made foundational contributions to what would become a Catholic-based liberation theology, especially in the critique of capitalist development, the call for structural revolution, and the warnings against U.S. imperialism.

Elsa Tamez

Another Methodist, Mexican-born theologian Elsa Tamez (b. 1950) is among the few to show how sexism is a major form of oppression. Using the Hagar story from Genesis, she illustrates how those women who are disenfranchised usually suffer under three forms of oppression: race, class, and gender. During the height of political repression in Latin America, many liberation theologians, who were mainly men, avoided controversial issues such as women's ordination. Missing from liberation theology was a feminist social critique. In the early development of liberation theology, one is hard-pressed to find women contributing to the discourse specifically as theologians. Those who did were usually relegated to Mariology, or a stereotypical celebration of motherhood.

In 1985, twenty-eight women gathered in Buenos Aires to share papers on liberation theology from the perspective of women. These papers appeared in the book *Through Her Eyes*, which was edited by Tamez. In another of her books, *Against Machismo*, Tamez interviewed the leading male liberation theologians and asked them if the oppression of women in Latin America existed. While all the interviewees thought it did, few provided a comprehensive analysis of the situation. The importance of *Against Machismo* is summed up in Tamez's own words: "Now we know there is a journey to be undertaken."[6]

Backlash

Liberationist thought started to develop in the midst of repressive governments. From the Rio Grande to Cape Horn, countries experienced military coups (with U.S. help), while existing governments shifted to the right, institutionalizing violence to maintain control. The Medellín Conference of 1968 was an attempt to implement the teachings of Vatican II to this context. What arose is what today we call liberation theology. The official church teaching that emerged from Medellín quickly spread throughout Latin America, thanks in part to the training programs and seminars conducted by the Latin American bishops' conference (CELAM). Not everyone, however, was happy with this new direction of theological reflection.

Belgian Jesuit Roger Vekeman, who years earlier while in Chile channeled $5 million from the CIA to help Eduardo Frei secure the presidency of Chile from 1964 to 1970,[7] established the Center for the Study of Development and Integration in Latin America (CEDIAL) in Bogotá, Colombia, and aimed to organize resources to oppose liberation theology. Joining him was Bishop Alfonso López Trujillo, who founded a journal titled *Tierra Nueva* (*New Earth*) to attack liberation theology. By cultivating the Vatican and

other Latin American bishops, and riding a genuine backlash from many moderate bishops, López Trujillo was able to capture CELAM by being elected in 1972 as its secretary-general. From this position, he immediately dismantled the proliberationist training programs and purged those who advocated liberation theology at CELAM, replacing them with more conservative staff and teachers.

Both Vekeman and López Trujillo saw liberation theology as supporting Marxist revolutions by reducing Christianity to the realm of politics. Their opposition to liberation theology on the basis of its perceived Marxist orientation did not make them procapitalists. Vekeman called for Christian socialism to avoid the evils of Marxism and capitalism, while López Trujillo saw capitalism as "a human failure."[8] They hoped to counter capitalism with a return to church orthodoxy and hierarchical authority.

Ten years after the Medellín Conference, López Trujillo hoped to delegitimize liberation theology by calling for a new conference in Puebla, Mexico (CELAM III), where he and his allies hoped to provide an alternative theology with a new set of symbols. Although supporters of liberation theology were shut out of the proceedings, they were nevertheless able to play crucial behind-the-scenes roles. The conference was delayed until 1979 because of the death of Pope John Paul I.

The conclusion of the Puebla Conference left no winners. In addition to those who advocated for liberation theology and those who called for its demise, there was a larger group comprised of centrists who, while concerned with the unity of the church, were also concerned with the defense of human rights. The Puebla Conference did not condemn liberation theology as it was designed to do; rather, as journalist and human rights activist Gary MacEoin observed, it ended up ignoring it.[9]

During this time, a newly elected pope, John Paul II, began to denounce some of the tenets of liberation theology, even while he spoke against social, political, and economic injustices. During a 1983 Central American tour, he engaged in a shouting match with Nicaraguans attending a Mass who were pressuring the pope to say a word concerning the atrocities being committed by the U.S.-backed contras. Instead, the pope seemed to endorse the archbishop, Miguel Obando y Bravo, who opposed the Sandinista government.

The pope's hatchet man, Cardinal Joseph Ratzinger, was appointed in 1983 as prefect of the Congregation for the Doctrine of the Faith. From this post, Ratzinger launched a systematic persecution of liberationists. In his own words, "With the analysis of the phenomenon of liberation theology, we are clearly facing a fundamental danger for the faith of the church."[10]

In early 1984, Ratzinger began making allegations to Gustavo Gutiérrez's supervisors concerning his unorthodoxy,

specifically Gutiérrez's supposed wish to replace the Catholic Church with the people's church. These accusations led to Gutiérrez's being summoned to the Vatican to explain himself.

That same year, Ratzinger went after other liberation theologians. He investigated Jon Sobrino for possible unorthodoxies and removed Clodovis Boff and six other priests from their teaching posts. Also in 1984, Ratzinger summoned Leonardo Boff to the Vatican to give an account for his accusations in *Church: Charism and Power* concerning the Vatican's authoritarianism. The Vatican ended up prohibiting Boff from teaching or publishing for one year. Boff eventually left the Franciscan order and continued to teach and write. The Vatican also attempted to silence a leading supporter of liberation theology in 1988, Bishop Pedro Casaldáliga of Brazil, and warning letters went out to eight of Brazil's progressive bishops. Not surprisingly, the silencing or attempted silencing of liberationists only created greater demand for their work, thus spreading their teachings beyond Latin America. In September 1984, Ratzinger wrote a thirty-five-page letter ("Instruction on Certain Aspects of the Theology of Liberation") listing the major objections to liberation theology. In reality, the letter condemned a caricature of liberation theology.

In spite of Ratzinger's dogged pursuit, the most effective strategy employed was the naming of conservative bishops in Latin America, who aggressively dismantled the work of earlier progressive bishops. Also, conservative cardinals (López Trujillo, for example) were appointed who, in turn, elected Ratzinger pope upon the death of John Paul II. Ironically, liberation theology survived persecution at the hands of the church because of the legitimization it

obtained during its persecution by repressive governments. The willingness of many liberationist church leaders to stand in solidarity with the oppressed even as they faced death preserved, more so than their writings, their theological work.

CHAPTER FIVE

Liberation in *El Norte*

We would be mistaken in assuming that liberation theology started in Latin America and then spread to North America. If liberation theology is rooted in how the oppressed theologically reflect on the liberative actions in which they are engaged, then a liberationist movement has always existed among the disenfranchised in North and South America. As we have seen, liberation theology is not a commodity that can be imported into different geographical areas. If liberation theology is contextual, we must carefully examine the different liberation theologies formed in *el norte*, the North. The question is not which came first, or which manifestation of the theology influenced the other;

rather, the question is this: How do these different liberation theologies coexist with and strengthen each other?

In August 1975, twenty-five Latin American liberationists met in Detroit with about 175 North Americans to discuss the significance of liberation theology within the United States. This conference, titled "Theology in the Americas," explored liberationist theological reflections from the perspective of the global South, recognizing that even in the heart of the United States, areas of the "global South" exist. The gathering was organized by Sergio Torres, a Chilean exile from Maryknoll, New York, who served as its executive secretary. Unfortunately, U.S. marginalized groups (i.e., blacks, hispanics, feminists, and Asian-Americans) were excluded from planning the event, leading to problems before it even began.

Among the North Americans who attended the Detroit Conference were members of U.S. disenfranchised communities, specifically feminists, African-Americans, Latino/as, and Asian-Americans. While different U.S. marginalized groups might share commonalities in their struggle against the imposition of a dominant Eurocentric theological 'norm;' there also existed dissimilarity that seemed to pit groups against each other, due mainly to the unexamined biases held by fellow participants at the conference.

Feminists pointed out to the Latin Americans how their work ignored the gender issue, specifically the oppression of women. African-Americans, on the other hand, were concerned about the lack of racial analysis in the work of these Latin Americans. In return, the Latin Americans were critical of both groups for taking the focus off the poor and failing to do rigorous economic analysis. They said that this was especially true of U.S. Latino/as, who seemed to focus more on cultural rather than economic analysis. They challenged feminists for not examining their white middle-class

privileges. Women of color were quick to point out that while their white sisters failed to scrutinize their racism, ethnic and racial brothers failed to scrutinize their sexism. It seemed that those oppressed in certain situations benefited from oppression in other situations. Some groups struggling for their own voice remained voiceless (i.e, lesbians, gays, bisexuals, and transgendered folks), absent from the table. Robert McAfee Brown captured well the dynamics of the conference: "Each group could point more skillfully to the mote in someone else's theological eye than to the beam in its own, and the corporate self-correction in these matters was immensely fruitful."[1]

Participants recognized the need to continue the conversations begun in Detroit. Some believed that the dialogue would be enhanced if Africans and Asians were invited to the table. To that end, Torres organized the Ecumenical Association of Third World Theologians (EATWOT), which held its first conference in 1976 in Dar es Salaam, Tanzania. In the next chapter, we will explore the globalization of liberation theology; however, for purposes of this chapter, we will focus specifically on U.S.-based liberationist theological perspectives. Before we do, it is important to remember that the theologies we are about to explore are not simply subsets of Latin American liberation theology but are liberative theological manifestations that arose from distinct contexts and experiences.

U.S. Feminist Theologies

During the 1960s, a new feminist theology developed that, like Latin American liberation theology, began to retrieve elements of Christianity that had been ignored by the dominant theological voices. Philosophers such as Simone de Beauvoir of France influenced the feminist movement by capturing the reality of androcentrism and demonstrating how being male becomes normative for all humanity. The enterprise in which early feminist religious thinkers partook was not easy. They were up against a Christian patriarchy comprised exclusively of male theologians, ministers, and even a male deity. They challenged how Christianity had come to legitimize and normalize male superiority within the faith.

It would be simplistic to reduce U.S. feminism to a monolithic expression. Several types exist. For example, liberal feminists focus on equal rights; cultural feminists emphasize the moral superiority of women and the traditional values women are associated with, like compassion or nurturing; radical feminists are concerned with male dominance and the problems it causes; and socialist feminists recognize the role played by class within capitalist societies. While different forms of feminism exist, there is agreement on the task of empowering women to move beyond harmful stereotypes and to work against oppressive social structures.

Just as different types of feminism exist, so too can feminist theology be grouped as revolutionary, reformist, or reconstructionist. Revolutionary feminist theology is influenced by radical feminism and advocates a post-Christian system that turns toward goddess traditions. Many conclude, as did Mary Daly, that Christianity is irredeemably patriarchal and beyond reform. "If God is male," Daly

quipped, "then the male is God."[2] Even though the church has had a centuries-long history of not treating women as equal human beings, Daly argued that if women's liberation is to succeed, it must encompass a religious vision—but that the vision should not be primarily Christian.

Reformists, on the other hand, do not advocate abandoning Christianity, but reforming it by questioning the established role to which the church and society have relegated women. Reconstructionists may agree with the reformist commitment to Christianity, but they find the reformist response to patriarchy insufficient. They make a liberationist call to transform both the faith and society. Not surprisingly, many reconstructionists are liberationist feminists.

Liberationist feminists do not make apologies for Christianity's patriarchy, but they do recognize that within the faith are liberative gems that can be used to dismantle the structural patriarchy and androcentrism of the faith and society. They call for a repentance that rights the life-denying wrongs caused by sexism. According to Ann M. Clifford, the methodology employed has three steps:

> 1. Attending to experience(s) of patriarchy and androcentrism by listening attentively to one's experience and that of other women and/or subjugated men; 2. Bringing these experiences into dialogue with a feminist reading of the Bible and/or other Christian texts; 3. Developing strategies for transformative action or praxis that are liberating.[3]

Below are a few early feminist scholars who raised the consciousness of Christians in hopes of a more inclusive faith.

Elizabeth Cady Stanton was an abolitionist prior to the U.S. Civil War and one of the original champions for women's suffrage. Arguing that organized religion and the Bible

were detrimental to women's personhood, she and a committee of twenty-six women wrote a biblical commentary titled *The Woman's Bible*.

Elisabeth Schüssler Fiorenza rereads the biblical text and other historical materials to reveal that women were active in the early church as apostles, theologians, ministers, missionaries, and prophets. For her, this liberating impulse of Christianity was tamed by Paul to make the new faith more appealing to surrounding communities through a process of "patriarchalization."

Phyllis Trible also provides a biblical reading that goes against the patriarchal grain. Centuries of reading the Bible with patriarchal eyes has created misogynist scriptural interpretations that reinforce the subordination and commoditization of women. Employing a hermeneutics of suspicion (suspicious of how the biblical interpretation supports the unexamined assumptions of those in power), Trible is able to reveal how men read their theology and gender biases into the text to justify the prevailing social structures that provide male privileges.

Rosemary Ruether is among the most prolific writers on the theme of liberation theology and feminism. Understanding that all language for God is not to be taken literally, but metaphorically and analogically, she rejects making the prevailing gendered image of God normative. God is beyond gender; hence, to insist on an unconditionally masculine God, or even a post-Christian Goddess, borders on idolatry. For Ruether, a liberative feminism develops a theology that critiques the tradition by pointing out how the tradition has harmed and limited women, that recovers women's stories to reveal their wisdom and insight in the doing of theology, and that revises and reshapes the tradition so that it can be more liberative for all church members, women as well as men.

bell hooks points out that feminist theory emerged from the social location of white, privileged women devoid of any knowledge or awareness of the life experiences of women and men who live on the margins; hence, there is a need for a theoretical expression rooted in the social location of non-white, under-privileged women.

While feminists are leery of importing a Latin American liberationist methodology to their North American context, so too are Latin American women and women of color concerned about universalizing Eurocentric middle-class feminism, as if North American feminism is the legitimate norm for all women of the world. Women of color have spoken on and written about their need to respond to the sexism within their own communities and to the racial, ethnic, and class prejudice within Anglo feminist communities that ignore the fundamental ways white women benefit from the oppression of women of color. Latin American women (as well as women from U.S. communities of color) are not necessarily interested in a male-female strategy that weakens a unified struggle for liberation from oppressive structures; likewise, these same women remain concerned with the men in their communities who dismiss white feminism as a Eurocentric project incongruent with the ethos of particular communities.

Unfortunately, for many disenfranchised men, any problems women face will be dealt with in some indefinite future once liberation is won for the community. Many men within marginalized communities may want to deal with sexism superficially (as in fighting for equal rights) rather than considering the depth and challenges brought forth by feminist theologians, specifically their critique of patriarchy.

Black Theologies

Blacks in North America endured almost 250 years of slavery, plus a century of segregation. The black American experience has been marked by violence, terror, brutality, and death. Since the first slaves were sold in the Virginia colony, however, a spirit for freedom has existed. This quest and hope for liberation can be traced to luminaries such as Nat Turner, Frederick Douglass, Harriet Tubman, Sojourner Truth, W.E.B. Du Bois, and Howard Thurman. But just as potent in the development of contemporary black liberation theology are the narratives of unknown or barely known men and women of faith who lived during brutal times— individuals such as Lewis Hayden, a Kentucky slave who after escaping oppression founded Bethel A.M.E. Church in Detroit and worked with the American Antislavery Society; or Samuel Ringgold Ward, who also escaped slavery,

became a pastor, wrote an autobiography, and aided and abetted fugitive slaves; or even Margaret Garner, an escaped slave who before being recaptured in Cincinnati, chose to kill her daughter rather than see her return to slavery. This slave religion emphasized God's immanence, ecstatic mysticism confirming God's presence, and secret gatherings to pray, share struggles, and wrestle with God. The transformative nature of God's word become foundational for the future development of black theology.

Slave religion, with its remnants of African spirituality, emphasized a worldview in which no delineation existed between the sacred and the secular. The slaves' suffering at the hands of white masters and overseers negated the spirituality these same whites claimed in the sacred spaces of church meetings. Whites exchanged Christ's message for a heretical plantation theology. As slaves became Christians, they rejected white interpretations of the Bible that stressed obedience to masters for stories like the exodus, in which God sides with the slaves and leads them out of the bondage of Egypt.

The civil rights movement of the 1950s and '60s was led by Christian liberationists such as Martin Luther King Jr. and Muslim liberationists such as Malcolm X, although, as the well-known saying reminds us, King didn't stand up until Rosa Parks sat down. On December 1, 1955, Parks refused to give up her seat on a public bus in Montgomery, Alabama, to a white man. This led to a citywide bus boycott and to the larger movement for civil rights.

King stressed that African-Americans can achieve freedom because God, working through black churches, stands in solidarity with them in the midst of individual and collective pain and suffering. He knew that segregationist laws contradicted the message of Jesus Christ, and he held up a mirror to reveal white America's religious hypocrisy. This was possible because black churches were radicalized. Their members protested, marched, conducted sit-ins and kneel-ins, and broke laws nonviolently (civil disobedience) as expressions of faith.

Malcolm X sought the liberation of colonized minds. As he said, "The worst crime the white man has committed has been to teach us to hate ourselves."[4] Unlike King, though, Malcolm X's nationalist message left open the option of using violence—"by any means necessary"—to obtain liberation. Although the two disagreed on strategy, they, along with countless women and men, both sought liberation as God's people while claiming their blackness. Ironically, both King and Malcolm X held low opinions of each other during their lifetimes; nevertheless, black theology encompasses the

radical gospel message of justice called for by King and the black power nationalism advocated by Malcolm X.

This theology of liberation was developing and maturing in North America just as an indigenous liberation theology was developing in Latin America. Although the spiritual quest for physical freedom can be traced back to the first slave ship (ironically named *Jesus*) that arrived in the New World, probably the birth of the modern concept of black theology can be dated to July 31, 1966, when the National Committee of Negro Churchmen (NCNC) published a full-page ad in the *New York Times*. For the first time, this manifesto declared to white America the relationship between the good news of the liberation found in Jesus and the oppressive reality experienced by black America. For black theologians and religious leaders, God's will was for them to be free from racism and from the social structures it undergirded, so that God's people could fully become the people they were created to be.

In 1969, James H. Cone published his classic book *Black Theology and Black Power*, which synthesized King's call for the black church to become radical institutions for social change and Malcolm X's call for black self-love. For Cone, Jesus Christ's call for liberation was congruent with the exercise of power within white America by African-Americans. Not only did Jesus the liberator stand in solidarity with blacks struggling for liberation, but this struggle signified the gospel in the twentieth century. By the creation of the Society for the Study of Black Religion in 1970, black theology had become an official academic discipline.

The development in the mid-1980s of "womanist" thought by black women pastors and theologians contributed to both feminist and black theology. The term was coined in the 1970s by Alice Walker, author of the book *The Color Purple*, as a wordplay on the pejorative word *woman-ish*, which refers to assertive and audacious black women who do not fit the role to which society has relegated them. *Womanist* instead celebrates such women as confident, dependable, and mature leaders who make valuable contributions to the whole community and who expand the discourse to include issues of gender and sexual orientation. Stephanie Mitchem defines womanist theology as "the systematic, faith-based exploration of the many facets of African-American women's religiosity . . . based on the complex realities of black women's lives."[5] Salvation is understood as ultimate liberation from all that enslaves.

Below are a few African-American scholars who have set the discourse for racial justice.

James H. Cone is considered one of the earliest black liberation theologians. He argues that white theology and the white God it represents are satanic because their historic acts of enslaving and oppressing black people are contrary to the liberating message of Jesus Christ. If Jesus calls for liberation, and the oppressed are black, then Jesus must be a black Christ who is found among the oppressed. For whites to be saved, they too need to believe and to follow an ontologically black Christ. Such a belief would be manifested in the dismantling of white racism.

J. Deotis Roberts, a political theologian influenced by King's nonviolent philosophy and the ideas of the black power movement, seeks "a Christian theological approach

to race relations that will lead us beyond a hypocritical tokenism to liberation as a genuine reconciliation between equals."[6] He attempts to balance Jesus' call for liberation with Jesus' call for reconciliation. He calls for a black Messiah (albeit a metaphorical one) to counter the psychological damage caused by whites who created a Christ in their own image before whom blacks must bow.

Jacquelyn Grant was among the first to accuse black theology of ignoring black women. Black theology could never be liberative as long as black women, who represented the majority in black churches, continued to suffer invisibly. For her, African-American women suffer under the three-pronged reality of sin: sexism, racism, and classism. Jesus as cosufferer, not surrogate, creates a space where he and the oppressed can share in each other's pain. Grant pointed out how the symbol of Jesus has been captured in the construction of white, male, and class privilege to justify and perpetuate existing social structures.

Employing a Marxist critique, *Cornel West* raised the concern that unless black theology seriously considered economic oppression, it would be irrelevant. Central to black theological conversations must be the plight of poor black people shut out of wealth and opportunities. Black theology must thus incorporate a democratic socialist approach.

In 1985, *Katie Cannon* was the first person to use *womanist* as a new category for African-American religious discourse. She is also responsible for writing the first text on womanist thought, *Black Womanist Ethics*, which makes black women's existential reality the arbitrator of ethical controversies. Using oral tradition and the experience of common people, Cannon rejects a Eurocentric ethics that makes white men's perspectives the norm in favor of an ethical survival strategy based on a hermeneutical suspicion

of dominant educational systems. Such an approach seeks to unmask structural racism, classism, and sexism.

For theologian Dwight Hopkins, the question black theology attempts to answer is this: What does it mean to be black and Christian? Because the black community is not monolithic, the question is answered in multiple ways. But however the question is answered, the black community, especially the church, plays a crucial role in working toward the liberation and humanization of African-Americans.

Hispanic Theologies

Contrary to popular opinion, Latina/o liberation theologies are not outgrowths of Latin American liberation theologies. While obvious similarities exist—for example, language and an overriding concern for justice—different contexts create distinct theological expressions. Although congruent with Latin American liberation theology, Hispanic theologies still stand apart by focusing more on culture than economics.

While the roots of Hispanic-based theologies can be traced to before the establishment of the United States, the most modern manifestation of these theologies took place in the 1970s and focused on the social location to which U.S. Latino/as were relegated. Four events contributed to the resurgence of Hispanic theologies: the 1971 founding of Las Hermanas, an organization dedicated to working with Latino/as in the fields of health, education, and pastoral services; the 1972 establishment of the Mexican American Cultural Center, which focused on pastoral services, research, and publication; the 1981 publication of *Apuntes*, the first Hispanic scholarly religious journal; and the 1988 creation of the Academy of Catholic Hispanic Theologians of the United States (ACHTUS).

Latino/a theologies do not come from a monolithic group. Among Hispanics, much of how a particular theology came to be constructed depends on the geographical location of its developers within the United States and on that group's nation of origin and its race or ethnicity (African, Indian, European, Asian, or a combination thereof). Consequently, the terms *Hispanic* or *Latino/a* serve as artificial demographic umbrellas grouping diverse constituencies from Spanish-speaking backgrounds under one label.

Despite this diversity, certain theological concepts resonate among Latino/as. One example is the concept of *lo cotidiano*, translated as "the everyday." Theology is conducted from *lo cotidiano* and focuses on the daily existence and struggles of Hispanics by critically analyzing the good and the bad that shape and form daily life. *Lo cotidiano* shifts the conversation away from the abstract and toward the flesh-and-blood reality of the marginalized. To understand the everyday recognizes that Hispanic-Americans live on the hyphen that serves as a seesaw between *Hispanic* and *American*. To be Latina/o is to live on the border, with one foot in the third world and another in the first. This is not just the physical border that separates the United States from Latin America, but invisible borders in every U.S. city and community that separate power from disenfranchisement, privilege from dispossession, and whiteness from "colored." To live on the borderlands is to exist in *nepantla*, the Aztec word for being in the middle. To live on the border, in *nepantla*, is to recognize the mixing, the *mestizaje*, of Hispanics, in which they belong and yet are not accepted because they lack purity due to ancestries that contain multiple racial and ethnic groups.

The liberationist theology that emerges is a survival theology whose purpose is to ascertain the character of God in the midst of Latina/o trials and tribulations, a character that provides guidance for what type of praxis the Hispanic community can undertake. However, any praxis must be done *en conjunto*, that is, within community. Moving away from the Eurocentric hyperindividualism that undergirds how theology has normatively been conducted in ivy towers, Latina/os commit to a collaborative methodology conducted within, by, and for the overall community. This becomes a praxis-centered theology of *acompañamiento*, of accompanying. It is through *acompañamiento* that a preferential option is made for those who are oppressed. To accompany becomes the praxis of being present alongside disenfranchised Hispanics.

Below are a few early Latina/o scholars who carved out a space within the academy for a Hispanic liberationist perspective.

Orlando Costas, a Puerto-Rican Baptist pastor-scholar, is considered among the first Protestants to shape the field of Hispanic theology. An evangelical, he was concerned with proclaiming the Reign of God, understood as a life-giving social order, to places where death and oppression reign. Salvation thus requires personal and structural transformation. To claim salvation while maintaining indifference to death-dealing social orders is to live a contradiction.

Mexican-American *Virgilio Elizondo* served as a priest in the San Antonio archdiocese and is considered among the first Catholics to shape the field of Latino/a theology. In his book *The Galilean Journey*, Elizondo developed the concept of *mestizaje*, miscegenation, as a theological lens from which Latino/as do theology. Jesus, like Latina/os today, is seen as a *mestizo*, as one rejected as impure by the religious and political powers. The miracle of the incarnation is not that God became human, but that God was incarnated among the disenfranchised and dispossessed—that God became a *mestizo*. Likewise, the Virgin of Guadalupe did not appear to the *mestizo* Juan Diego as a white European, but as a *mestiza* who spoke his indigenous language. The future of theology in the United States is therefore *mestizo*. Elizondo is also credited with founding the Mexican American Cultural Center (MACC).

María Pilar Aquino, a Mexican and former nun in the Society of Helpers, was among the first to use the concept *lo cotidiano* as a response to sexism and the male-oriented dominance of liberationist thinkers. Her work forced liberationists who were advocating for political liberation to seriously consider their complicity with sexist structures. She held that it is in the everyday lived experience of women that the confluence of the private and public occurs.

Justo González is a Cuban Methodist historian. For him, the Trinity, which represents co-equality among the Deity,

becomes a paradigm for society to emulate. God is incarnated as a Jesus who, like Hispanics, lives in poverty. Not only is the Deity understood through the social location of Hispanics, but so too is the biblical text, which is read from the perspective of marginality, poverty, *mestizaje*, exile, and solidarity. González is the founding editor of *Apuntes*, as well as three institutions that promote Latina/o presence within the academy: the Association for Hispanic Theological Education (AETH), the Hispanic Theological Initiative (HTI), and the Hispanic Summer Program (HSP).

Ada María Isasi-Díaz, a former Cuban Catholic nun in the Order of St. Ursula, used the term *mujerista* to name the theological reflection conducted by Latinas. Her work advocated a methodology that recounts the story of women, analyzes their reality, develops new expressions of worship, and seeks means for empowerment. For her, the Bible was not the source of liberation for Hispanic women; rather, they draw from the tradition of popular religious devotions. Although popular religious devotions may provide deep wisdom in times of trouble, not all Latinas are willing to dismiss the biblical text or refer to themselves as *mujeristas*. Most Hispanic women prefer the term *feminista*, as demonstrated in the edited volume *A Reader in Latina Feminist Theology: Religion and Justice*.

In the 1990s, Hispanic theology experienced a boom as newer Latino/a scholars obtained doctorates and published books. Nevertheless, Hispanics remain grossly underrepresented within the academy and the church, even though they represent the largest U.S. ethnic group.

Asian-American Theologies

When most people in the United States consider Asian-American religious expressions, they think Buddhist, Hindu, or Taoist. They fail to understand that most people within this second-fastest-growing group in the United States are Christians, and they fail to account for the diversity within the Asian-American community. Asian-Americans comprise diverse nationalities, cultures, languages, and migration patterns. Although the presence of Asians in North America can be traced to the sixteenth century, the Asian population (specifically Chinese) began to grow in earnest in California during the 1848 gold rush. Unfortunately, many encountered discriminatory policies and violence, which culminated in the "Yellow Peril" that scapegoated Asians for "stealing American jobs." These racist sentiments led to several Chinese immigration exclusion acts, starting in 1882. Shutting the door to the Chinese exacerbated the need for labor in the West, which consequently encouraged Japanese,

Korean, and Filipino migrants to come to the United States. Not surprisingly, they too faced similar prejudices.

In 1924, all Asian immigration was legislatively curtailed. In 1942, months after the Japanese attack on Pearl Harbor, President Franklin D. Roosevelt signed Executive Order 9066, which forcibly seized the assets of Japanese-Americans and relocated them to ten concentration camps until the war's end—even while young Japanese men were fighting on behalf of the United States in Europe. German-Americans and Italian-Americans did not face similar treatment. After the Second World War, immigration policies were loosened, culminating in the 1952 Nationality Act. This act reopened Asian immigration, although quotas still restricted access. This changed in 1965 with the Immigration and Nationality Act, which abolished the quota system.

Ironically, Asians in the United States have been labeled by whites as a "model minority," able to relatively succeed in spite of race or ethnicity and thus proving that the American Dream is available to anyone willing to work hard. Regardless of the media hype, Asian-Americans, like other minority groups, are disproportionately disenfranchised and are quickly marginalized if they threaten the privilege of the dominant culture. Regardless of how many generations their ancestors have lived in the United States, physiognomic features such as eye shape relegate all Asian-Americans to being "forever foreigners."

No normative Asian-American theological perspective exists. Asian-Americans come from very different national origins, and within each national group are diverse cultural groups. Nevertheless, some common theological concepts, contextualized in the real-life experiences of Asian-Americans, resonate with most of the group.

Marginality has led Asian-Americans to suffer unbearable generational injustices. Experiences of multiple marginalities

caused many to develop an inexpressible feeling in the pits of their stomachs. The Korean community names this pang *han*. *Han* encompasses the feelings of resentment, helplessness, bitterness, sorrow, and revenge that are felt deeply in the victim's guts and that become the daily companion of the powerless, the voiceless, and the marginalized. *Han*, however, is not restricted to the individual. When social injustices prevail throughout the whole community for several generations without an avenue of release or cleansing, a collective *han* develops. For many Asians, or those of Asian descent, life in the United States is a *han*-ridden experience.

Religious pluralism, more common in Asia, is also an important theme among Asian-American liberationist theologies. To accept one religion does not necessarily require rejecting or demonizing other religions. Hence, Asian-American theologies are more hybrid than those of Western Christianity. Eastern religious traditions—for example, reverence for ancestors—coexist with Christian practices.

Confucius believed that the greatest virtue was *hsiao* (filial piety) and that it was the first principle of heaven and the ultimate standard by which people are to conduct their lives. In a time of societal breakdown, marked by intellectual dogma, moral uncertainties, and political instability, Confucius turned to *hsiao* as a way of restoring harmony and promoting family values. *Hsiao* encourages family reunions at ancestral shrines and support to bereaved family members both financial and emotional. In effect, *hsiao* is a deep-rooted expression of devotion that reaffirms the basic understandings of family duty, obligation, values, and responsibility. Most who participate in *hsiao* are not seeking blessings, protection, or guidance from the deceased through some form of supernatural powers; rather, they are connecting earthly care for family elders with their spiritual well-being. Hence, there is a distinction between worshiping ancestors as deities and participating in a ritual that links the living presence of the dead with the consciousness of the bereaved.

Many early Asian-American Christian scholars developed a liberative faith understanding based on their social location. Among them are the following.

Choan-Seng Song is a Taiwanese scholar best known for his advocacy of story theology, the usage of non-Christian parables, folktales, and fairy stories to inform a Christianity that is part of a pluralistic world. He also suggests using a "third eye" theology. To open a third eye is to be open to that which has previously gone unseen due to one's ignorance. A third eye allows Christianity to turn to the abundant indigenous stories, legends, and folklore of the people. These stories serve as authentic symbols by which Asians practice their faith. Through these indigenous stories, transmitted from generation to generation, consciousness is raised about the power of love, humanity, justice, and morality.

Jung Young Lee, a Korean Methodist, was among the first to develop an Asian-American theology of marginality,

which was based on his experience of living on the margins between America and Asia, where he was in between (neither American nor Asian) and in both worlds. Liberation is only possible, he said, if the dominant culture is liberated from its biases, prejudices, and exclusivity.

Roy Sano, a Japanese-American Methodist, was theologically influenced by his internment during World War II. As founder and director of the Pacific and Asian American Center for Theology and Strategies (PACTS), he advocated church involvement in civil and human rights movements. Eventually serving as the first Japanese-American bishop in the United Methodist Church, Sano's influence was mainly due to his leadership roles.

David Ng is a Chinese-American Presbyterian theologian who advocated for an inclusive and multicultural church sensitive to plurality, diversity, and the bonds of solidarity that unite all believers. The unique cultural traits of the Asian community are celebrated as God's gift to the overall faith community for the betterment of Christian communion. Through a narrative theology based on his experience of being born to an immigrant family that suffered ethnic discrimination, he refused to reject his cultural context. Instead, he sought to synthesize his Christianity with his Confucian traditions.

Kosuke Koyama lived in Japan during World War II. His experience informed his struggle to remain faithful to his faith while struggling against satanic forces operating in the name of the Christian God. During his missionary days in Thailand, he sought to indigenize the Christian faith by focusing on the everyday experiences of Asians. Relying on an autobiographical methodology, he attempted to

understand the biblical tradition through the Buddhist culture of Asia.

Although the contributions of Asian-American liberationist scholars are ignored by many theologians, their focus on multiple marginality and multifaith theological methodologies has contributed greatly to liberationist theology and has helped it to move away from a strictly Western discourse. Theology rooted in an Asian context facilitates the consideration of a liberation spirituality that is not solely rooted in Christianity, a concept to be explored more carefully in the next chapter.

CHAPTER SIX

The Faiths of the People

In Zimbabwe, a young man is beaten to death for disagreeing with the government. In Thailand, a young girl is sold into prostitution so her family can eat. In Palestine, a family continues to be trapped in the cycle of dispossession. Outrage over injustices and suspicion concerning dominant structures is not limited to the Americas. Most of the world's inhabitants live under some form of repressive structures, be they cultural, political, economic, or religious. Whenever those relegated to nonpersonhood turn to their faith for direction in the struggle against their disenfranchisement, they are accessing the spiritual liberative resources found within their religion, regardless of whether that religion is or is not Christian. Whenever spiritual forces and theological reasoning are mustered in search of fostering right relationships within a fractured world, we can argue that a liberative turn was made within the religion.

One of the main claims of Latin American liberation theologians has been their insistence that they are articulating the theological reflections that first emerged from the grassroots faith community. Yet these reflections at times appear to be very Western and Catholic. When we consider that most of the poor are a mixture of races and cultures, we are left to wonder where the indigenous elements of the

faith of the people are incorporated. Some would argue that a very Catholic and Western liberation theology is destructive to indigenous cultures, that it participates in colonizing a discourse that is hostile to native peoples. Often missing from liberation theology is the reflection of the religious faith of the poor, whose beliefs are shaped by their own spirituality.

While liberation theology may historically be rooted in a Christian (mainly Catholic) tradition, liberative theologies are found within the faiths and spirituality of all people. This chapter will explore how this liberative spiritual impulse is expressed in other geographical and religious locales. We will see both the manifestation of Christian-based liberation theology throughout the world and the manifestation of liberative theological perspectives within other world faith traditions.

Abrahamic Traditions

Islam

As the central figure within Islam, the prophet Muhammad demonstrated a preferential option for the disenfranchised. He displayed great sympathy for orphans, widows, outcasts, and the poor, and he warned converts to stay away from the wealthy and powerful. He was fond of saying, "My poverty is my pride." Not surprisingly, Islam's first converts were those from the humbler class. Upon arriving at Madinah, Muhammad's party was called *muhajirs*, an Arabic word that refers to immigrants or outsiders. The Prophet, who came from among the poor, participated in a revolutionary quest to liberate the social conditions of his time by challenging the power structures of the wealthy in Mecca.

The Qur'an ties true worship (2:43, 83) and true repentance (9:5, 11) with the paying of the *az-zakah*. The *az-zakah* is obligatory charity due from all Muslims for the poor. Its purpose is to purify the human soul from the vices of greed, stinginess, covetousness, and lustfulness, while providing comfort to the dispossessed by meeting their needs. *Az-zakah* is meant to offer protection for the weak from the oppressive economic reality of usury (2:276), and from the powerful who wish to devour the property of the weak (2:29; 4:2). Those who exploit the poor are classified by the Qur'an as disbelievers (4:37; 9:34–35). Additionally, the Qur'an demands economic justice (55:8) as implied in the word *jihad*, which entails a struggle against wealth (4:95).

Within Muslim tradition are seeds for creating a society on earth that reflects Allah's justice. For example, the pre-Islamic Arabian value of personal honor encouraged generosity, even to the point of slaughtering one's last camel. Muslims are commanded to give *sadaqa*, emphasizing discretion for the recipient's feelings (2:271). *Sadaqa* can be translated as a voluntary charity, a concept expressed as any act of giving based on the believer's compassion, love, or generosity.

Besides the *az-zakah* and the *sadaqa*, one of the Five Pillars of Islam is the *zakat*, the giving of alms. The believer is required to give a small percentage of his or her possessions to charity, generally to the poor and dispossessed. The concept serves as a type of welfare contribution to disenfranchised Muslims. The *zakat* stresses generosity (9:60). In addition to the *zakat*, the faithful are obligated to perform the *zakat al fitr* (fast-breaking almsgiving) at the conclusion of Ramadan (2:184). The practice is connected with the pillar of *Sawm* (fasting in Ramadan) and acts as a purification of the fast itself. This preferential option for the poor is also demonstrated during the Eid al-Adha, the festival of

sacrifice commemorating the willingness of Abraham to sacrifice his son as an act of obedience to God. According to tradition, two-thirds of the feast meal is for family, friends, and neighbors, and one-third is reserved as a gift for the poor.

Among the leading contemporary Muslim liberative thinkers are Asghar Ali Engineer (India) and Ali Shari'ati (Iran). Engineer is among the first to explore the intersection of liberation theology and Islam. He believes that Sufism, which is closer to the heart of the people, serves as a corrective to the more orthodox and rigid legalism of mainline Islamic traditions. He argues that the historical traditions of the faith, specifically the life of the Prophet, the teachings of the Qur'an, and the Sunnah (traditions and examples) of the Prophet, contain liberative elements of egalitarianism. Shari'ati sees the Qur'an as advocating socialistic ideas. While Islam and Marxism differ on ideology and strategy, both share a concern for social justice.

In Islam, all are equal before Allah—*la bedawi fil Islam* (there is no bedouinism in Islam). Because bedouins are nomadic Arabs who live in tents, the phrase stresses that in Islam, neither caste systems nor lineages exist. A concerted effort is made to dispel racism and classism, as illustrated by the two unstitched white clothes worn during the *haj*. During the *haj* (the fifth pillar of Islam), all who journey to Mecca wear the same cloth regardless of wealth or lack thereof. Prince and pauper worship Allah side by side with no indication of rank or status. A true celebration of diversity occurs during the *haj* that, for a time at least, overcomes barriers of caste, class, and color.

Allah is never unjust (4:40); rather, Allah demands justice (7:29; 49:9; 5:8) and forbids oppression, which is why numerous Qur'anic exhortations command believers to fight for the cause of the oppressed (4:74–76). The ideal Islamic government can best be modeled on the caliph Abu Bakr's words: "The weak among you is strong in my eyes until I get justice for [them] . . . and the strong among you is weak in my eyes until I exact justice from [them]."[1]

Judaism

Most Christian liberation theologians returned to their Jewish roots in the Hebrew Bible to serve as the hermeneutical foundation of liberationist thought. The story from Exodus of a God who enters history to liberate God's chosen (preferential option) from the bondage of Egyptian slavery and leads them toward the promised land has become a major biblical motif in the construction of liberation theology. Just as important is the message of the prophets, which ties the will of God with a call to defend society's most vulnerable members. In the time of the prophets, these were the widows, the orphans, and the aliens. Jews, who are seen as Isaiah's suffering servants, are called to stand in solidarity with the least of these who also suffer. To accompany those who suffer is a paramount praxis that undergirds any understanding of Jewish theological or ethical thought. Standing in solidarity with the oppressed recovers and re-embraces the prophetic consciousness found within the Jewish prophetic traditions.

Although Christians and Jews share the liberative seeds found in the Hebrew Bible, the development of a Jewish theology of liberation is more than simply biblical. One of the leading Jewish liberative thinkers, Marc Ellis, moves the discourse beyond the survival narratives of the biblical exodus and the twentieth-century Holocaust to deal with the ethical concerns presently facing Jews. Specifically, he is concerned with the expansionism demonstrated by the State of Israel. While Jewish empowerment to prevent another Holocaust is important, it can neither override injustice nor be achieved at the expense of another community. The oppressed cannot become the new oppressors. For this reason, he calls Jews to embrace the Palestinians and their cause.

Suffering of Jews during the Holocaust resonates with other marginalized and disenfranchised communities today throughout the world, providing an opportunity to develop a more inclusive approach to theology. Jews of consciousness confront "Constantinian Judaism" by creating a world where no group suffers oppression as did the Jews, especially at the hands of Jews. Hence, Jewish identity since the Holocaust cannot be equated with Zionism; Judaism (like any other religion) cannot be used to justify oppressive

structures. The misuse of power by the State of Israel toward the Palestinians betrays previous Jewish suffering and oppression. A call for a theology of solidarity to replace a theology of the Holocaust is therefore advocated. True Jewish identity is found through solidarity with the oppressed of the land, whether they be Jews during the Holocaust or Palestinians today.

Palestinian-Christian Liberation Theology

Izdat Said Qadoos, a poor Palestinian villager, probably said it best: "[Born-again Christian evangelicals] are filled with ideas that this is the Promised Land and their duty is to help the Jews. It is not the Promised Land. It is our land."[2] Qadoos's sentiments resonate with the misery and hardship faced by many displaced Palestinians. In response to Palestinian marginalization, Christian Palestinians created a grassroots movement rooted in the Jesus narrative to deal with their dispossession and disenfranchisement. Palestinians living on a land occupied by others relate to a Jesus who also lived on occupied land. Using Jesus as a model, they seek reconciliation and a just peace through a two-state solution that guarantees Israel's security and Palestinian self-determination. For a two-state reconciliation to occur, Palestinians must recognize the Holocaust and Israel's right to exist, while Israel must acknowledge the oppression it has inflicted on Palestinians and work toward the abolition of its nuclear arsenal.

A leading Palestinian liberation theologian is Naim S. Ateek, an Anglican priest and founder of the Sabeel Center in Jerusalem. *Sabeel*, Arabic for "the way," is an ecumenical organization that seeks to promote unity among Palestinians through social action based on love, justice, peace, and nonviolence. Additionally, Palestinian liberation theology

attempts to counter the misuse of the Bible by Christian Zionists that provides theological justification for the displacement of Palestinians based on the belief that the Jewish temple must be rebuilt on the Temple Mount in Jerusalem, where an Islamic mosque, the Dome of the Rock, presently sits. Jesus' second coming, according to this eschatology, cannot occur until the temple is rebuilt for Jesus to take possession. Regardless of what action the State of Israel takes, regardless of how unjust it may be, Christian Zionists normatively view it as God's will. The unquestioning marshaling of resources for Israel by these mainly conservative and evangelical Christians is directly responsible for the forced exile and continuous oppression of Palestinians.

But before these Palestinians can advocate for a liberation theology, there must first be a liberation of theology. For these reasons, a de-Zionization of the Bible is needed. For example, rejecting the exclusive notion of a chosen people allows for a theological call that before God there is no Jew or Gentile. All are equal, with no one group holding special claims to any type of promised land, especially when the land was already occupied, whether by the Canaanites in biblical times or the Palestinians today.

Asian Traditions

Minjung

To stand in solidarity with those who are suffering and those who are oppressed demonstrates the appropriate action for *minjung*. *Minjung* is a Korean Christian liberationist response that developed during the rise of industrialism and the oppression with which it was associated. An untranslatable word made up of two characters (*min*, which means "people," and *jung*, which means "mass"), it refers to the common folk, those who are not of the ruling elite. Minjung theology is the liberative theology of the colonized, those who are economically, politically, sexually, and socially oppressed. They bear *han*, the generational suffering that results from unjust experiences.

Yet it is those abandoned by Korean history who are the true subjects of that history and are responsible for developing a new consciousness. The search is on for subjects who transform their times, then and now, through liberative communities rooted in justice. *Dan*, understood as experience of the divine, counters *han* by leading toward liberationist acts with the potential of transforming the individual and the world. Korean colonial history and its multireligious context are reexamined through *minjung* eyes to see God's presence in the people's struggle for justice. Hence, theology becomes the sociobiographical story of *minjung* history, in which Jesus is discovered as one with the *minjung* of his time. To see God moving within Korean history (salvation history) confirms God's movement in contemporary political situations.

Stories of oppression become the foundation for rereading the history of Asians and understanding what praxes are required for liberation. While Korean Christians may lean more toward an exclusive conservatism, minjung theologians are quick to include non-Christian faith perspectives, narratives, stories, and tenets in their theological reflection. In true liberative fashion, it emerges from the grassroots in their struggle for liberation, and it is rooted in a Korean social context that unapologetically incorporates indigenous shamanistic traditions.

Suh Nam-dong was the first to use the term *minjung* in relationship to theological thought in a 1975 article titled

"Theology of *Minjung.*" The theology and movement of *minjung* developed in the 1970s as a Christian response to the dictatorial reign of Park Chung-hee. As Christian leaders and missionaries took jobs in industrial centers as an act of solidarity with workers, they discovered harsh conditions and abuses. Learning the *han* of *minjung* informed how they read their Bibles and how they conceptualized their theology. From their *minjung* experiences and daily struggles, a *minjung* theology developed. They discovered that the gospel could neither be preached nor understood apart from the *han* of *minjung.*

Buddhism

The Buddha's teachings of the Four Noble Truths recognize that there is suffering caused by desire and cravings. This suffering can be overcome by following the Noble Eightfold Path of right understanding, intention, speech, action, livelihood, effort, mindfulness, and concentration. Because of the interrelatedness of all life, liberation from suffering and compassion for all who suffer are central concerns of Buddhism. Engaged Buddhism becomes a communal praxis by which these concerns are met, while recognizing the independency of the causes of suffering. Important in the demonstration of compassion are the *sangha*, or Buddhist-based communities that provide villagers not only with Buddhist teachings but also with education, medical help, and occupational advice. A dhammic socialism, which is the political ideology of socialism constructed upon the principles of Buddhism, is established, revolving around the belief that no one should take more than what is needed.

Buddhists argue that the source of human suffering can be combated if attention is given to eliminating the ignorance, fear, hate, and greed (the major reasons why poverty and scarcity exist) that lurk in all human hearts. In this way, the ultimate goal of achieving emptiness, understood as *nibbana* or *nirvana* (synonymous with happiness, peace and liberation) can be achieved. All have a right to the opportunity of achieving *nirvana*. For such an opportunity to exist, four levels of freedom are prerequisite: (1) physical freedom, in which basic needs (food, clothing, shelter, health care) are met; (2) social freedom, consisting of a lack of oppression, injustice, exploitation, and violence; (3) emotional freedom, which is fostered by love, happiness, compassion, and generosity; and (4) intellectual freedom, which is based on a wisdom absent of biases, distortions, or unexamined ulterior motives.

By denying the ego, the reality of the totality is affirmed. Awareness, via meditation, of the shortcomings of one's own ego leads to less emotional investment in it and thus more capacity for compassion. During the Vietnam War and the Tibetan protests of Chinese occupation, Buddhist monks have immolated themselves to show compassion for the suffering and to be in solidarity with the victims for the fight of freedom and liberation. Buddhist social actions should seek to achieve the ideal Buddhist social order, decentralized and respectful of local culture while void of poverty and with self-sufficiency as the norm (except for the monks). The overriding concern would be how the reduction of desire (consumerism), coupled with compassion for others, can be applied to global problems to create the conditions in which each person has the opportunity of achieving *nirvana*.

Buddhist Vietnamese monk Thich Nhat Hanh links the interconnection of all living beings with peace and social justice by raising people's consciousness of their personal behaviors in relation to the larger community. He stresses an "inter-being" that advocates an enlightenment that leads to a transformation of the self and the other, rather than an enlightenment based on the abstract. Through mutuality and collaboration, the truth that nurtures justice can be unlocked. He summarizes his understanding of what justice may look like: "If you have compassion, you cannot be rich. . . . You can be rich only when you can bear the sight of suffering. If you cannot bear that, you have to give your possessions away."[3]

Hinduism

Hinduism has been called fatalistic due to the concept of *karma*, which appears to blame a victim's marginalized station on destructive past lives. Nevertheless, *karma* might be better understood as a liberative concept which insists that all actions have moral consequences, not solely in some future reincarnated life, but also in this life. The goal of life in Hinduism is *moksha* (or *mukti*), which means ultimate liberation. While *moksha* refers to a release from the cycle of reincarnation, some Hindu thinkers have reinterpreted it to refer more to life in this world. *Moksha* strives for release from the existential human dilemma of estrangement while remaining keenly aware of divine mystery. The obstacle to achieving *moksha* is *karma*, or self-centered actions. Although human estrangement can be remedied through asceticism, meditation, and/or the pursuit of the ethical, *moksha* remains a divine gift of grace. The Vedas (the earliest Hindu scriptures) teach that liberation is harmony with fellow humans, the cosmos, and the divine. Because order within the cosmos is a prerequisite to human well-being, assistance from *divas* (superior beings who are custodians of the cosmic order) is needed. The ideal society is imagined as *ramrajya* (kingdom of Rama), which is free from the suffering caused by poverty.

While partial liberation can take place on this earth, the entire cosmos is moving toward full liberation, which is integrated within divine life. For the individual human, reaching this goal may require several life cycles. What prevents full liberation, according to the Upanishads (later Hindu scriptures), is *avidya*, an ignorance requiring riddance so that the human spirit, awakened to its true self, can unite with *Brahman*, the absolute. This unity moves the heart toward divine love (*bhakti*), which motivates the self toward liberative acts. Other liberative concepts can be found in the Bhagavad Gita, which recounts the dialogue between Krishna (the incarnation of the god Vishnu) and Arjuna before an epic battle that symbolizes the lifelong

struggle between justice (*dharma*) and injustice (*adharma*). The Gita teaches that in the midst of such cosmic struggles over justice, all that can be done is to surrender to the Divine (2,7), for liberation is awareness of the unity of the human self with the divine self (13,25) free from egotistical cravings (2,48).

One of the best-known liberative Hindus was Mahatma Gandhi, who believed in many different paths to the divine life. His development of *swaraj*, or liberation, became the central theme of his lifelong work to end British colonial rule in India. In advocating *swaraj*, Gandhi was calling for a system of home rule that rejected all forms of exploitation and oppression (not simply British) and that tolerated different faith traditions. *Swaraj* was to be achieved through *satyagraha*, or the clinging to truth, understood by Gandhi as God. The struggle for truth occurred through a nonviolent praxis of passive resistance and civil disobedience against unjust and discriminating laws. A major component to *satyagraha* was *ahimsa*, or nonviolence. India's independence was to rest on three pillars: (1) economic self-sufficiency, hence the call to daily hand spinning; (2) liberation for the least within society, specifically women and the so-called untouchables; and (3) harmony and unity between Muslims and Hindus. By demonstrating his service to others, Gandhi exhibited the path to God. As he said, "The service of the distressed, the crippled and the helpless among living things constitutes worship of God."[4]

Dalit Theology

The Sanskrit word *dalit* means "broken" and refers to those broken by Hindu's caste system, which is based on a hierarchical order determined by ritual purity and pollution. The pinnacle of the social hierarchy is occupied by scholars and priests (*Brahmins*), followed by the warriors who govern (*Kshatriyas*), then those engaged in commerce (*Vaisyas*). At the bottom are workers, servants, and peasants (*Shudras*). Beyond this social order (out-caste) is a group known as the untouchables, or Dalits, who are considered polluted and unclean because they deal with unclean or polluted objects in their jobs. Even their gods and goddesses serve the higher deities of those who are not untouchable. Though the caste system was abolished in 1950, the Dalits—whose numbers exceed 200 million, or 20 percent of India's inhabitants (according to the International Dalit Solidarity Network)—still face oppression and discrimination. Three millennia of oppressive social structures cannot simply be eradicated through modern laws. Hence, any liberative Dalit religious thought, regardless of its religious affiliation, must focus on sociocultural liberation.

Conversion to other faiths became a means of seeking liberation for many Dalits. Those who left Hinduism for other faiths in the hopes of escaping the discrimination of the caste system found that even in non-Indian-based faiths such as Christianity or Islam, the caste system was still accepted as a social reality. A pioneering Dalit Christian, Arvind P. Nirmal, took the image of Jesus as the suffering servant of Isaiah and saw a Dalit broken and forsaken on the cross. Also important for Dalit liberative thought is the concept of the banquet table set by Jesus (Mark 2:16–17) where the outcast, the Dalit, is invited to partake.

Others have found liberation within Buddhism, as in the case of the Dalit Panther community, which synthesizes

Buddhist and Marxist thought. Still others remain in Hinduism, claiming an older (*asi*) Hindu egalitarian tradition that is anti-caste and anti-ritual, over against the prevailing elitist hierarchy. Among the leading figures advocating a Hinduism of one caste to which all humans belong was Mahatma Gandhi, who proclaimed, "If we are all children of the same Creator, naturally there cannot be any caste amongst us."[5]

Philosophical Traditions

Humanism

Among the first liberationist thinkers to move away from basing human hope solely on the transcendent is Rubem Alves, a Brazilian credited with being one of the earliest contributors to liberation theology. He advocates a "political humanism" that looks toward a better tomorrow based on the human dimension, rather than on a divine hand that leads from the ethereal realm. For Alves, humans are historical beings; as such, they must become the subject, rather than the object, of history.[6] Because hope is historical, Alves envisions an end to the inhuman social structures that exist; hence, one must continue to hope for their end. However, it is humanity, not God, that will bring about human justice. Alves can be understood as advocating a theistic humanism that calls for human responsibility manifested as justice causing praxis within the context of a divine reality. A synergism is created between God's presence in human history and human accountability and responsibility in enacting liberative praxis.

Leading African-American humanist thinker Anthony B. Pinn can be understood as a proponent of naturalistic humanism, which is less concerned with the divine, focusing instead on any significance that theological or religious thought might have on humanity. For Pinn, the belief in Jesus Christ's redemptive suffering is harmful because all suffering is bad, especially for the oppressed. He calls for a "strong humanism" because any God who supports suffering as beneficial is not good news for the marginalized. Metaphysical reality is thus met with suspicion as this-worldly self-reliance becomes the means toward life fulfillment. If the bases for humanism are respect and dignity for humans, then seeking justice becomes a humanist imperative because of the inhumanity of oppressive structures. Liberative justice and human progress are not achieved through supernatural intervention, but through human hands.

Other American Traditions

The primacy of Eurocentric and Catholic thought in the original development of Latin American liberation theology is self-evident, even though one of the main claims has been their insistence that they are articulating the theological reflections emerging from the grassroots faith communities— communities that, for the most part, were indigenous. When we consider that most of the poor in Latin America are a mixture of races and cultures, we are left wondering where the indigenous and African elements of the faiths of the people are incorporated. Some argue that a very Catholic and European liberation theology is destructive to indigenous and African-based cultures, that it participates in "colonizing" a discourse that is hostile to indigenous people and people of African descent. Missing from Latin American liberation theology is the reflection of the non-Christian faith of the poor, whose beliefs are shaped by their indigenous or African cultures.

Native

Among Christian liberationists, one of the most powerful biblical stories is that of the exodus, in which God enters history and guides God's chosen people toward the promised land. The trek of former slaves toward liberation resonates with many who today are dispossessed. Unfortunately, we usually ignore the fact that this promised land was already occupied by the Canaanites, who first had to be slaughtered (Josh. 6:21) before God's chosen could take possession. While most marginalized Christians read themselves into the story of the oppressed slaves marching forward, many indigenous people see themselves as the modern-day Canaanites.

The Hebrews'/Europeans' dream of religious freedom and liberation became the Canaanites'/Amerindians' nightmare of subjugation and genocide. Like the Canaanites before them, Indians were viewed as a people who could not be trusted, a snare to the righteous, and members of a culture that required decimation. Robert Allen Warrior provides a rereading of the exodus story from the Canaanite perspective, questioning if it is an appropriate biblical model for understanding his people's struggle for dignity.[7] He calls for a Christian reflection that places the Canaanites at the center of theological thought and that considers the violence and injustice rarely mentioned in critical works concerning the book of Exodus.

Leading Native American scholar George "Tink" Tinker argues that even though Christian missionaries may have had the best of intentions, their religious attempts to "Christianize the heathens" contributed to the oppression of the indigenous people and eventually led to their downfall. It is important to recognize that those who brought the gospel to Indians did so at a terrible cost. Individuals such as Bartolomé de las Casas (Catholic) or Henry Benjamin Whipple (Protestant), heralded as defenders of the Indians, still contributed to their ultimate annihilation, in spite of heartfelt convictions and good intentions. Las Casas was responsible for creating the "reduction" paradigm for missionary conquest, which physically separated Indians from their families and communities, while Whipple engineered the stealing of the Black Hills from the Sioux nation, bringing an end to their resistance.

Scholars such as Vine Deloria Jr. are quick to remind us that Latin American liberation theology is as oppressive to Indian people as the former theologies of the colonizing missionaries. The conquest of Indian land by "God's chosen

people" ended the Indians' liberation, understood as communal and personal harmony and balance. Hence, any discussion of liberation among indigenous people must be understood as liberation from European Christian invasion and its consequences. These consequences are evident today when we consider that American Indians are the poorest of the poor in a Christianized North America, a poverty maintained by systematic oppressive structures that politically, socially, psychologically, and economically suppress. Liberation among Indian people, according to Deloria and Tinker, begins with a firm "no" to Jesus Christ and Christianity, the source of Indian bondage. For them, liberation is focused on the ceremonial structures that promote a pre-1492 harmony and balance. A societal and political recentering of ancient ceremonies, along with their traditional communitarian value systems, restores a world-view of an intimate connection to the whole of creation.

African-based

Enslaved Africans brought their indigenous faith to the so-called New World. Many of those brought to the Caribbean and Brazil, who came from Yorubaland (present-day Nigeria) worshiped African quasi-deities known as *orishas.* To avoid religious persecution, slaves masked their *orishas* with the faces of Christian saints. This was a deliberate act (not syncretism) that allowed them to remain faithful to their quasi-deities, while avoiding punishment from their overseers for maintaining their homeland's religious traditions. For example, the religion Santería, which developed in Cuba, consists of an Iberian Christianity shaped by the Counter-Reformation and by Spanish "folk" Catholicism blended with African *orisha* worship. While the roots of Santería can be found in Africa's earth-centered religious practices, medieval Roman Catholic Spain, and European spiritism, it is neither African nor European. And while many elements of Santería can be found in the religious expression of Europe and Africa, it formed and developed along its own trajectory.

Different unique hybrids developed as the religious traditions of Yoruba slaves took root on different Caribbean soils. The vitality of Yoruba religiosity also found expression through Catholicism as Voudou in Haiti and New Orleans, Shango in Trinidad and Venezuela, Candomble in Brazil, and Kumina in Jamaica. *Orisha* worship is not limited to a Catholic-Yoruba hybrid religion, however. Examples of this African faith combining with Protestantism can be found in the Jamaican groups Revival and Pocomania. A similar example can be noted in the Trinidadian group known as Spiritual Baptists or Shouters, in which Yoruba faith finds expression through Christian fundamentalism.

Since their inception, these *orisha*-based religions have been an expression of a people's attitude toward finding harmony—harmony between oneself and one's environment, one's community, and the spiritual realm. For this reason, African-based religions as manifested in the Americas can only be understood through the disharmony caused by the social and political situation of the believer. During times of persecution, *orisha*-based religions have served and empowered a people to survive the adversity they were facing. In a

very real sense, they were created by the disenfranchised to protest their subjugation and to resist their annihilation.

Followers of the *orishas* seek harmony with the world (what is seen and unseen) and those with whom they share the planet. If harmony is maintained between heaven and earth, then those who dwell on earth experience enlightenment, prosperity, peace, and good health. If, however, disharmony and imbalance prevail, then ignorance, scarcity, violence, and malady will plague the earth. One asks the *orishas* for the power (*ashe*) to struggle efficiently against these oppressive forces, specifically in the areas of societal subjugation, physical diseases, and relational difficulties. Each believer is responsible for seeking the greatest good for the entire community, even when that good conflicts with what is best for the individual. Hence, selfishness is frowned upon.

Conclusion

When faith traditions access the liberative qualities of their religion, they can be understood as religions of resistance. As religions of resistance, they become a source of strength for a persecuted people who are searching for a means of survival while challenging the forces of oppression. Liberative interpretations of belief systems adhered to by marginalized and persecuted people render a counterhegemonic challenge to the prevailing social and political order. More than just means for the survival of their devotees, liberative religions of resistance provide the disenfranchised with a source from which to champion social change. Cultural resistance did not develop solely due to Latin American liberation theology; rather, it has always been an intrinsic component of the different faiths of the oppressed.

The best faith can offer is to provide a spiritual foundation from which the outcast, the voiceless, the nonhuman, can demand the dignity of their humanity. Liberative thought is not restricted to Christianity. I have more in common with my Muslim, Hindu, and Buddhist sisters and brothers operating from the liberative impulses of their faith than I do with other Christians complicit in the overall structures of oppression. Because most of the world's disenfranchised are non-Christians, any response to oppression, specifically in the form of state sponsorship of global capitalism, must involve people from various religions. If we argue that the greatest threat to human dignity is a savage militarized capitalism that dehumanizes people for the sake of profit and is accepted virtually as a faith; then the only hope of resistance for the world's disenfranchised may lie within their own faith traditions. Rather than religion being the opiate of the people, its more liberative interpretations might prove to be complicit in their salvation. The liberative impulse of the faith of the people, rooted in praxis, provides an alternative to the globalized religion of mammon known as neoliberalism.

CHAPTER SEVEN

Moving beyond
Liberation Theology

When liberation theology began to take shape in Latin America during the 1960s, there was hope that countries could move toward democratic socialism. Unfortunately, the power of economic globalization was underestimated. Since the collapse of the Berlin Wall, which signaled the triumph of capitalism and new growth opportunities for neoliberalism, liberation theology began to appear outdated. Military dictatorships gave way to elected civilian governments. With the collapse of communism and the election in Latin America of leftists and a few former revolutionary guerrillas to public office, some began to question the relevance of liberation theology. According to Ernesto Cardenal, the priest and former Nicaraguan Sandinista, "Liberation theology is in crisis. Capitalism won. Period. What more can be said?"[1]

The rise of neoliberalism has contributed to a series of economic and political changes, both in Latin America and elsewhere. Faced with a new world order, many of the original statements and discussions of liberation theologians in the 1960s and 1970s are no longer relevant to today's economic challenges. Some scholars, especially those from the dominant culture, began to view liberation theology as a fad, as no longer relevant. During a 1996 conference of the American Academy of Religion, Gustavo Gutiérrez proclaimed that he did not believe in liberation theology but believed in Jesus Christ. And even though all theologies are born to die, a theological voice emanating from the margins of society will always exist, regardless of what it is called.

While earlier liberationists used Marxist analysis to better understand the social location of the oppressed, more recently, thinkers are engaging postmodern, postcolonial, and queer theories as a way of better comprehending the plight of the marginalized. In this final chapter, we will move beyond liberation theology as it was defined in Latin America during the 1960s. Maybe the very term *liberation* needs to be liberated. The time may well have arrived when the 1960s' understanding of liberation theology has to die, and let the dead bury the dead.

If Gutiérrez's assertion is correct, then this book needs to conclude with an exploration of how theological perspectives are contemplated today from the margins of power and privilege. The theologies of the 1960s may have been important then, but they fall short in dealing with the world of today. For that reason, any liberative theology must change with each new generation to meet the latest manifestations of oppression faced by society's least. To that end, we will explore the contributions of a sampling of contemporary liberative thinkers and some of the overarching themes in which they work.

Rethinking Christian Base Communities

José Comblin, a Belgian who has been expelled from Chile and Brazil, was among the first to question how theology must change to meet the challenge of the new century, which is transforming the ethos of those oppressed in Latin America. He realized that the Brazilian poor were leaving the poverty of rural life and moving into urban areas in search of employment. This migration weakened the Christian base communities, which were already decimated by decades of repression. Despite their early success in outlying barrios, CEBs had never made much of an impact

TRADING SPACES...

among middle-class traditional churchgoers within the parish center or among the very poor of the city and surrounding countryside. Economic changes, as well as migration, have since brought the CEB movement to a standstill. Even people who continue to struggle for land now live in the city. Should they obtain land, they may work on it for a while, but they will inevitably return to the urban centers where many have discovered a greater measure of economic salvation.

Meanwhile, the rich have isolated themselves from their compatriots, moving to exclusive gated suburbs and hiring security guards for protection. While exclusion is not a new phenomenon, what is new is their abandonment of the lower middle classes, who remain trapped in the city with the incoming poor. The newly rich are no longer the old bourgeoisie *patrones* who may have felt paternalistic toward those under them. The new elite feel little obligation to the poor. For their part, the poor are no longer able to take advantage of the historical client relations of the *patron* structure.

An ironic quip heard among Latin American religious circles goes, "While liberation theologians made a preferential option for the poor, the poor made a preferential option for Pentecostalism." Philip Berryman, an American priest of Hispanic descent who ministered in Central America, does not see the future as belonging to the CEBs, which continue to decline. Instead, the future in Latin America belongs to *evangelicos* (not to be confused with U.S. evangelical Protestantism), particularly in its Pentecostal form. The explosive growth of these non-Catholic groups is contributing to a new religious reality in urban Latin America. The emphasis that some evangelical Protestant groups place on prosperity theology makes this new religious movement more compatible with the tenets of capitalism. This new religious focus on personal piety and prosperity is unlikely to challenge neoliberalism. For liberation theology to remain relevant, closer attention to neoliberalism needs to occur.

Rethinking Biblical Interpretations

Many Christian liberationists turn to the biblical narratives as a source for praxis; however, it cannot be denied that these texts have been used also to justify crusades, inquisitions, conquest, slavery, and other forms of oppressive systems. Through the use of postcolonial theories, scholars have begun to reread the biblical text, unmasking how its words are not always as liberating as we would hope. Biblical scholar R. S. Sugirtharajah of Sri Lanka is among the principal architects of a fairly new category of biblical studies called postcolonial criticism. Postcolonial criticism examines the complicity of Eurocentric biblical interpretations with the colonial phenomenon; specifically, it asks how the Bible has been used to enforce and reinforce colonial structures. To read the Bible with postcolonial eyes calls into question the relationship between the Bible, colonialism, and theology. Such a reading engages a discourse of resistance that challenges the ideologies and assumptions which historically have used religion to justify the colonizing venture.

In a similar vein, Fernando F. Segovia, a Cuban and the 2014 president of the Society of Biblical Literature, attempts to decolonize the Bible to explore the foundation of the contextual scriptural readings emerging from the theoretical, methodological, and sociocultural diversity found in marginalized communities. The hope of this view from the margins is to move closer toward a liberation also rooted in challenging the ideologies and assumptions of the colonizers. Kwok Pui-Lan, a Chinese scholar and the 2011 president of the American Academy of Religion, is also among those who have combined postcolonial theory and biblical hermeneutics to arrive at spiritual resources. She argues that because multiplicity and plurality are integral to

the Asian reality, the Bible should be read in dialogue with the ancient scriptures of Asia to avoid the superimposition of a Eurocentric framework on the development of Asian hermeneutics. Moving away from this Eurocentric normativity was best illustrated when Korean scholar Chung Hyun Kyung performed a ritual dance at the 1991 Assembly of the World Council of Churches in which she called upon the Holy Spirit through the spirits of the global victims of Christianity, ending with an invocation to the female bodhisattva of compassion, Guanyin.

Rethinking Praxis

Although it was obvious that several of the participants at the Detroit Conference held in 1975 were gays or lesbians, opposition to the oppression of lesbians, gays, bisexuals, and transgender people (LGBT) was not officially represented during the gathering. They may have been present, but they were invisible. To include their voices or perspectives would have been considered inappropriate, if not indecent. It is precisely this indecency that Marcella Althaus-Reed, an Argentinean, calls for as she seeks a sexual theology that can arise from liberation theology. The decency of liberation theology ignores how decency for women implies a complex set of sexual regulations, along with an oppressive web of expectations based on gender. Those most likely to be considered indecent are usually poor women of color. To counter this decency, she calls for the doing of theology with one's panties off. In other words, she calls for a move beyond what has been constructed as proper behavior, which in reality masks oppressive relationships. The "indecent theology" that she advocates is a theology which starts with people's experiences, void of any censorship. It is a theology that

147

tells people to come as they are, and to come out of the closets.

I am Miguel A. De La Torre, an exiled Cuban and the author of this book, and I also argue for an indecent approach to praxis. I believe that the global success of neo-liberalism makes any hope of liberation from oppressive economic systems unrealistic. The marginalized occupy the liminal space between the crucifixion of Friday and the resurrection of Sunday. To occupy Holy Saturday is a hopeless space where all that is known is the brutality and violence of Friday. Sunday remains uncertain, too far away to just wait for. To live in the space of Holy Saturday is to embrace the hopelessness of the moment. Those with middle-class privilege are too much in a rush to get to Sunday. What is needed is to sit with the disenfranchised in the dust, accompanying their suffering. To be hopeless is not to give in to fatalism. The oppressed have no choice but to continue fighting for the basic necessities, regardless of whether they are going to win or not. Only those living with middle-class privilege can throw their hands into the air and cry out, "Why bother?" The hopelessness in which the oppressed live propels them toward praxis. Here is the true liberative ethical question: Do we fight for justice because we know we will win, or do we fight for justice, regardless of the outcome, for the sake of justice alone?

What becomes the liberationist response in the face of neoliberalism, which probably will not be vanquished in our or our children's lifetimes? I have developed what I call an ethics *para joder* (an ethics that "screws with"). When the oppressive structures cannot be overturned, the only ethical response is to screw with the structures, to create disorder

and chaos. This is an ethics that employs the trickster image to upset the normative law and order of those in power who require stability to maintain their privileged position.

Get Out of Your Armchair!

Did you notice the irony that a book concerning the praxis-oriented religious movement known as liberation theology has the word *armchair* in its title? The very ethos of *being* a liberation theologian is the *doing* of liberation theology. Unlike most Eurocentric theological perspectives that place an emphasis on correct doctrine, liberationists are more concerned with correct action. One cannot *do* from the comfort and security of one's armchair. Liberationist theological thought can never be learned through books written by "experts" (this particular author included) residing in prestigious schools of higher education. As the Boff brothers remind us, "Such places are hardly the epicenters from which liberation theology emanates; its theologians are not armchair intellectuals, but rather 'organic intellectuals' (in organic communion with the people) and 'militant theologians,' working with the pilgrim people of God and engaged in their pastoral responsibilities."[2] Yet this very book elucidates liberation theology for those wishing to be and/or remain armchair theologians.

Liberation theology is not just another theological perspective struggling with ethereal concepts concerning eschatology or ecclesiology. Liberation theology is a critique of Western political, economic, and social structures from the perspectives of the disenfranchised. Oppression is a theological problem that requires the faithful not just to contemplate, but through praxis, to bring about justice. So why this book? Why spend the energy on explicating a movement to those sitting in comfortable armchairs? Because of hope that

in hearing the good news of liberation, you will leap out of your armchair and begin to actually do your theology. Hence, this book must end with a challenge. *See* the misery and hopelessness in which the majority of this world's people live, *judge* the prevalent global social structures responsible for so much of the world's poverty and repression, and *act* toward making changes that reflect your faith. This challenge is not because you expect or hope to overcome these structures and win, but because your faith calls you, pleads with you, to act.

Notes

1. Resistance!

1. Letter of Saint Polycarp, Bishop of Smyrna, to the Philippians 11:2, quoted in J. Philip Wogaman, *Christian Ethics: A Historical Introduction* (Louisville, KY: Westminster/John Knox Press, 1993), 27.

2. Catherine of Siena, *The Dialogue, The Bridge*, 33, quoted in Wogaman, *Christian Ethics*, 73.

3. Quoted in Thomas Kidmore and Peter Smith, *Modern Latin America* (New York: Oxford University Press, 1984), 18

4. Gustavo Gutiérrez, "Foreword," *Witness: Writings of Bartolomé de Las Casas* (Maryknoll, NY: Orbis Books, 1993), xi, 46–48.

5. George E. "Tink" Tinker, *American Indian Liberation: A Theology of Sovereignty* (Maryknoll, NY: Orbis Books, 2008), 11–12.

6. Pablo Richard, *Death of Christendom, Birth of the Church*, trans. Phillip Beryman (Maryknoll, NY: Orbis Books, 1987), 27.

2. Opening the Windows

1. Mark Kline Taylor, *Remembering Esperanza: A Cultural-Political Theology for North American Praxis* (Maryknoll, NY: Orbis Books, 1990), 134–35.

2. Deanne William Ferm, *Third World Liberation Theologies: An Introductory Survey* (Maryknoll, NY: Orbis Books, 1986), 9.

3. Quoted in William I. Robinson and Kent Norsworthy, *David and Goliath: The U.S. War against Nicaragua* (New York: Monthly Review Press, 1987), 56–57.

Notes

4. Jack Nelson-Pallmeyer, *School of Assassins: Guns, Greed, and Globalization* (Maryknoll, NY: Orbis Books, 2001), 2.

5. Quoted in Lisa Hauhaard, "Torture 101," *New York Times*, October 14, 1996.

6. Nelson-Pallmeyer, *School of Assassins*, 34.

7. Antony Jay, *Lend Me Your Ears: Oxford Dictionary of Political Quotations* (Oxford: Oxford University Press, 2010), 54.

8. Christian Smith, *The Emergence of Liberation Theology: Radical Religion and Social Movement Theory* (Chicago: The University of Chicago Press, 1991), 20.

9. Camilo Torres, *Revolutionary Priest: The Complete Writings and Messages of Camilo Torres*, ed. John Gerassi (New York, NY: Random House, 1971), xiii.

10. Ibid., 369.

11. Emilio A. Núñez C. *Liberation Theology*, trans. Paul E. Sywulka (Chicago, IL: Moody Press, 1985), 116.

12. Third World Bishops, "A Letter to the Peoples of the Third World (August 15, 1967)," in *Liberation Theology: A Documentary History*, ed. Alfred T. Hennelly (Maryknoll, NY: Orbis Books, 1990), 49–56.

13. Second General Conference of Latin American Bishops, *The Church in the Present-Day Transformation of Latin America in the Light of the Council* (Washington, DC: Division for Latin America, 1973), 14:I:1.

14. John Eagleson, ed., "Declaration of The 80," *Christians and Socialism: Documentation of the Christians for Socialism Movements in Latin America* (Maryknoll, NY: Orbis Books, 1975), 4.

15. Christian Smith, *Emergence of Liberation Theology*, 21.

3. Liberation Theologies: What Are They?

1. Sakiko Fukuda-Parr, ed., *United Nations Development Programme's Human Development Report 2003* (New York, NY: Oxford University Press, 2003), 8.

2. Leonardo Boff, "Vatican Instruction Reflects European Mind-Set (August 31, 1984)," in *Liberation Theology*, ed. Alfred T. Hennelly, 418.

154

4. Early Proponents

1. Quoted in Plácido Erdozaín, *Archbishop Romero: Martyr of Salvador*, trans. John McFadden and Ruth Warner (Maryknoll, NY: Orbis Books, 1981), 75–76.
2. Gustavo Gutiérrez, *The Power of the Poor in History*, trans. Robert R. Barr (Maryknoll, NY: Orbis Books, 1984), 51.
3. Leonardo Boff, Jesus *Christ Liberator: A Critical Christology for Our Times*, trans. Patrick Hughes (Maryknoll, NY: Orbis Books, 1978), 250.
4. Ibid., 53.
5. Juan Luis Segundo, *The Liberation of Theology*, trans. John Drury (Maryknoll, NY: Orbis Books, 1976), 7–8.
6. Elsa Tamez, *Against Machismo: Interviews by Elsa Tamez*, trans. John Eagleson (Yorktown Heights, NY: Meyer-Stone Books, 1987), 147.
7. "Religion: Cope-and-Dagger Stories," *Time*, August 11, 1975.
8. Arthur McGovern, *Liberation Theology and Its Critics: Toward an Assessment* (Maryknoll, NY: Orbis Books, 1989), xix.
9. Gary MacEoin, "American Synod, Rome Agenda," *National Catholic Reporter*, October 25, 1996.
10. Cardinal Joseph Ratzinger, "Liberation Theology (March 1984)," in *Liberation Theology*, ed. Alfred T. Hennelly, 367.

5. Liberation in *El Norte*

1. Robert McAfee Brown, "A Preface and a Conclusion," in *Theology in the Americas*, ed. Sergio Torres and John Eagleson (Maryknoll, NY: Orbis Books, 1976), xii.
2. Mary Daly, *Beyond God the Father: Toward a Philosophy of Women's Liberation* (Boston, MA: Beacon Press, 1973), 19.
3. Ann M. Clifford, *Introducing Feminist Theology* (Maryknoll, NY: Orbis Books, 2001), 35.
4. Quoted in James H. Cone, *For My People: Black Theology and the Black Culture* (Maryknoll, NY: Orbis Books, 1984), 159.
5. Stephanie Y. Mitchem, *Introducing Womanist Theology* (Maryknoll, NY: Orbis Books, 2002), ix.

6. J. Deotis Roberts, *Liberation and Reconciliation* (Philadelphia, PA: Westminster Press, 1971), 34.

6. The Faiths of the People

1. Quoted in Akbar S. Ahmed, *Discovering Islam: Making Sense of Muslim History and Society* (London, GB: Routledge & Kegan Paul Ltd., 1988), 33.

2. Quoted in Jim Rutenberg, Mike McIntire, and Ethan Bronner, "Tax-Exempt Funds Aiding Settlements in West Bank," *New York Times*, July 6, 2010.

3. Thich Nhat Hanh, *The Raft Is Not the Shore*, trans. Daniel Berrigan (Maryknoll, NY: Orbis Books, 1975), 102.

4. Quoted in Ignatius Jesudasan, *A Gandhian Theology of Liberation* (Maryknoll, NY: Orbis Books, 1984), 318.

5. Ibid., 78.

6. Rubem Alves, *A Theology of Human Hope* (Washington, DC: Corpus Books, 1969), 3.

7. Robert Allen Warrior, "A Native American Perspective: Canaanites, Cowboys, and Indians," in R. S. Sugitharajah, ed., *Voices from the Margin: Interpreting the Bible in the Third World* (Maryknoll, NY: Orbis Books, 1991), 277–85.

7. Moving beyond Liberation Theology

1. Quoted in Juan O. Tamayo, "Rethinking Option for Poor: Liberation Theology Barely an Echo in Old Stronghold," *Miami Herald*, January 31, 1999.

2. Leonardo Boff and Clodovis Boff, *Introducing Liberation Theology*, trans. Paul Burns (Maryknoll, NY: Orbis Books, 2001), 19.

For Further Reading

Primary Sources

Althaus-Reid, Marcella. *Indecent Theology: Theological Perversions in Sex, Gender, and Politics*. London: Routledge, 2000.

Alves, Rubem. *A Theology of Human Hope*. Washington, DC: Corpus Books, 1969.

Aquino, María Pilar. *Our Cry for Life: Feminist Theology from Latin America*. Maryknoll, NY: Orbis Books, 1993.

Boff, Clodovis. *Feet-on-the-Ground Theology: A Brazilian Journey*. Translated by Phillip Berryman. Maryknoll, NY: Orbis Books, 1990.

Boff, Leonardo. *Jesus Christ Liberator: A Critical Christology for Our Times*. Translated by Patrick Hughes. Maryknoll, NY: Orbis Books, 1978.

Bonino, José Miguez. *Doing Theology in a Revolutionary Situation*. Philadelphia: Fortress Press, 1975.

Cannon, Katie G. *Black Womanist Ethics*. Atlanta: Scholars Press, 1988.

Cone, James H. *Black Theology and Black Power*. New York: Seabury Press, 1969.

De La Torre, Miguel A. *Latina/o Social Ethics: Moving beyond Eurocentric Moral Thinking*. Waco, TX: Baylor University Press, 2010.

Deloria, Vine, Jr,. *Custer Died for Your Sins: An Indian Manifesto*. New York: Macmillan, 1969.

Elizondo, Virgilio. *Galilean Journey: The Mexican-American Promise*. Maryknoll, NY: Orbis Books, 1983.

Ellacuría, Ignacio, and Jon Sobrino, eds. *Mysterium Liberationis: Fundamental Concepts of Liberation Theology*. Maryknoll, NY: Orbis Books, 1993.

For Further Reading

Ellis, Marc H. *Toward a Jewish Theology of Liberation: The Uprising and the Future.* Maryknoll, NY: Orbis Books, 1987.

Engineer, Asghar Ali. *Islam and Liberation Theology: Essays on Liberative Elements of Islam.* New Delhi: Sterling Publishers, 1990.

Freire, Paulo. *Pedagogy of the Oppressed.* Translated by Myra Bergman Ramos. New York: Continuum, 1970.

Gutiérrez, Gustavo. *A Theology of Liberation.* Translated by Sister Caridad Inda and John Eagleson. Maryknoll, NY: Orbis Books, 1973.

Koyama, Kosuke. *Waterbuffalo Theology.* Maryknoll, NY: Orbis Books, 1973.

Kwok Pui-lan. *Postcolonial Imagination and Feminist Theology.* Louisville, KY: Westminster John Knox Press, 2005.

Lee, Jung Young. *Marginality: The Key to Multicultural Theology.* Minneapolis: Fortress Press, 1995.

Second General Conference of Latin American Bishops. *The Church in the Present-Day Transformation of Latin America in the Light of the Council.* Washington, DC: Division of Latin America—USCC, 1973.

Segovia, Fernando F. *Decolonizing Biblical Studies: A View from the Margins.* Maryknoll, NY: Orbis Books, 2000.

Segundo, Juan Luis. *The Liberation of Theology.* Translated by John Drury. Maryknoll, NY: Orbis Books, 1976.

Sobrino, Jon. *Jesus the Liberator: A Historical-Theological Reading of Jesus of Nazareth.* Translated by P. Burns and F. McDonagh. Maryknoll, NY: Orbis Books, 1993.

Sugirtharajah, R. S. *Asian Biblical Hermeneutics and Postcolonialism: Contesting the Interpretations.* Maryknoll, NY: Orbis Books, 1998.

Tamez, Elsa. *Against Machismo: Interviews by Elsa Tamez.* Translated and edited by John Eagleson. Oak Park, IL: Meyer-Stone, 1987.

Introductory Texts

Amaladoss, Michael. *Life in Freedom: Liberation Theologies from Asia.* Maryknoll, NY: Orbis Books, 1997.

For Further Reading

Berryman, Phillip. *Liberation Theology: Essential Facts about the Revolutionary Religious Movements in Latin America and Beyond.* Philadelphia: Temple University Press, 1987.

Boff, Leonardo, and Clodovis Boff. *Introducing Liberation Theology.* Translated by Paul Burns. Maryknoll, NY: Orbis Books, 2001.

Clifford, Anne M. *Introducing Feminist Theology.* Maryknoll, NY: Orbis Books, 2001.

Cohn-Sherbok, Dan. *World Religions and Human Liberation.* Maryknoll, NY: Orbis Books, 1992.

De La Torre, Miguel A., ed. *Handbook of U.S. Theologies of Liberation.* St. Louis: Chalice Press, 2004.

————, ed. *The Hope of Liberation in World Religions.* Waco, TX: Baylor University Press, 2008.

De La Torre, Miguel A., and Edwin David Aponte. *Introducing Latino/a Theologies.* Maryknoll, NY: Orbis Books, 2001.

Ferm, Deane William. *Third World Liberation Theologies: An Introductory Survey.* Maryknoll, NY: Orbis Books, 1992.

Hennelly, Alfred T., ed. *Liberation Theology: A Documentary History.* Maryknoll, NY: Orbis Books, 1990.

Hopkins, Dwight N. *Introducing Black Theology of Liberation.* Maryknoll, NY: Orbis Books, 1999.

McGovern, Arthur. *Liberation Theology and Its Critics: Toward an Assessment.* Maryknoll, NY: Orbis Books, 1989.

Mitchem, Stephanie Y. *Introducing Womanist Theology.* Maryknoll, NY: Orbis Books, 2002.

Pedraja, Luis G. *Teología: An Introduction to Hispanic Theology.* Nashville: Abingdon Press, 2003.

Smith, Christian. *The Emergence of Liberation Theology: Radical Religion and Social Movement Theory.* Chicago: University of Chicago Press, 1991.

Tan, Jonathan Y. *Introducing Asian American Theologies.* Maryknoll, NY: Orbis Books, 2008.

Index

Abraham, 115–23
abundant life, the,
    1–2, 19–20,
    42–45, 57
acompañamiento,
    103, 149
Africa
    and liberation
        theology, 35,
        123–33, 137–
        39
    and oppression of,
        55, 74, 137
    people of, 15, 18,
        88, 101, 113,
        134
    spirituality of, 94,
        137–39
African-American,
    46, 86, 93–100,
    132
Alexander VI, Pope,
    7
Allah, 116, 118–19
Althaus-Reed, Mar-
    cella, 147
Alves, Rubem, 132
Aquino, María Pilar,
    104
Arbenz, Jacobo,
    17–18, 22
Argentina, 25, 74,
    76, 78, 147

Asia
    and liberation
        theology, 35,
        123–32, 147
    oppression of, 55,
        74, 110, 124
    people of, 45, 88,
        101, 106–12
Asian-American, 45,
    86, 105–12
Asian-American the-
    ologies, 105–12
Assmann, Hugo, 39
Ateek, Naim S., 121

Baker, Lorenzo Dow,
    16
Bakr, Abu, 119
bananas, 16–18
Batista, Fulgencio,
    28
Beck, Glenn, 41–42,
    53
Belgium, 79, 143
Berryman, Philip,
    145
Bhagavad Gita, 128–
    29
Bible, 11–13, 28,
    41–43, 47,
    49–50, 53–54,
    57, 59, 62,
    66–67, 70–71,

75–76, 78,
    90–92, 94–97,
    105, 112, 119,
    122–23, 125,
    131, 134–35,
    145–47
black liberation
    theology, 42,
    93–100
Boff, Clodovis,
    68–69, 82, 150
Boff, Leonardo, 39,
    54, 60, 66–69,
    71, 82, 150
Bolivia, 25, 29
Bonaparte, Napo-
    leon, 15
Bonino, José
    Miguez, 76–77
Brazil, 26, 30, 33,
    35–36, 39, 66,
    68, 82–83, 132,
    137, 143
Buddhism, 105, 112,
    125–27, 131–32,
    140

Cabrera, Manuel
    Estrada, 16
Cámara, Hélder, 26,
    35
Canaanites, 123,
    134–35

Index

Cannon, Katie,
99–100
capitalism, 21,
29–30, 39,
56–57, 59–60,
76–77, 80, 89,
140–42, 145,
148–49
Cardenal, Ernesto,
142
Casaldáliga, Pedro,
82
caste system, 118,
130–32
Castro, Fidel, 28
Catherine of Siena,
3–4
CELAM, 30–31,
79–81
Central Intelligence
Agency (CIA),
18, 22, 24, 79
Chile, 38, 79, 86,
143
China, 18, 106, 111,
127, 146
Christendom, 6–10,
14–15, 18–19,
28, 32, 34, 57–58
Christian base com-
munities, 26–28,
36, 61, 143–45
Christianity
atrocities of, 2,
4–14, 89–90,
95, 135–36,
140, 147
churches of, 1–4,
6–10, 14–16,
18–19, 25–36,
38, 42, 47,
57–59, 61, 64,
66–73, 75–77,
79–84, 90–91,

93–96,
99–100, 103–
5, 109–11,
121, 145
as liberative, 4–5,
9–10, 95,
109
See also Christen-
dom
Chung Hyun Kyung,
147
civil rights move-
ment, 18, 95–96,
110
classism, 2–4, 14–16,
30, 36, 51, 57,
61, 78, 86–87,
89, 92, 99–101,
115, 118, 144,
148–49
Clifford, Ann M., 90
Colombia, 34, 37,
45, 79
colonialism, 2, 5–18,
24, 32, 60, 74,
95, 115, 123,
129, 134–35,
143, 145–46
Columbus, Christo-
pher, 7, 9
Comblin, José, 143
communism, 18, 26,
28, 39, 76, 141.
See also Marxism
*comunidades eclesiales
de base* (CEB). *See*
Christian base
communities
Cone, James, 42,
97–98
Confucius, 108–9,
111
conquistadores,
5–14, 16–18

consciousness, raising
of, x, 19–20, 27,
36–37, 44, 47–
48, 59, 63, 90,
109, 123, 127
contextual theology,
33, 35, 44–46,
49, 53, 71, 76,
79, 85, 88, 92,
101, 107, 111–
12, 124, 132,
146
conversion. *See* Jesus
Christ: conversion
to; salvation
Cortés, Hernán, 8
Costas, Orlando, 103
cotidiano, lo. See
everyday, the
crucified people,
51–52, 64, 72
Cuba, 21, 28–30, 39,
60, 62, 104–5,
137, 146, 148

Dalit, 130–32
Daly, Mary, 89–90
D'Aubuisson, 25
d'Auxerre, Guil-
laume, 3–4
de Beauvoir, Simone,
88
de Las Casas, 9–14,
135
De La Torre, Miguel
A., 148–50
Deloria, Vine, 135–
36
del Valle, Juan, 10
de Medellín, Diego,
9
democracy, 18, 22,
29, 31, 99, 141
dependency theory,

15–16, 19, 21,
23–24, 28–29, 55
Detroit Conference,
86–88, 147
de Valdivieso, 9–10
Douglass, Frederick,
93
Du Bois, W.E.B., 93
Dussel, Enrique,
74–75

Eisenhower, Dwight,
18
Elizondo, Virgilio,
103
Ellacuría, Ignacio, 73
Ellis, Marc, 119–20
El Salvador, 25,
63–64, 71, 73
encomienda, 10, 13
Engineer, Asghar Ali,
117–18
ethics *para joder*,
149–50
ethnic discrimination,
51, 87, 92, 100–
107, 111
eurocentric theology,
14, 16, 44, 47,
49, 51, 54, 60,
86, 92–93, 95,
99, 103, 134,
145, 147, 150
Europe, 6, 13–14,
16, 18, 30, 55,
70, 74, 79, 101,
104, 107, 134–37
everyday, the, ix–x,
26, 43, 50, 60,
64, 67, 101–2,
104, 111

feet-on-the-ground
theology, 68–69

feminism
Euroamerican, 86,
88–93, 97
Latin American,
78, 92–93
and women of
color, 87,
92–93, 97, 99,
104, 105, 147
Fiorenza, Elizabeth
Schüssler, 91
Fort Benning, Geor-
gia. *See* School of
the Americas
Frei, Eduardo, 79
Freire, Paulo, 36–37

Gandhi, Mahatma,
129–30, 132
Garner, Margaret, 94
genocide, 5–6, 8,
13–14, 56, 134–
35
God
anti-, 19, 43, 98,
111, 132
character of, 3, 8,
11, 43, 49, 53,
58, 64, 94,
103–4, 111,
117
gender of, 88–90,
92
imago Dei (image
of God), 13,
44
of the oppressed,
37, 45, 49–51,
58–59, 64, 72,
95, 104, 119,
124, 134, 150
reign (kingdom)
of, 52–53, 67,
76, 103

understanding of,
49, 59, 70–71,
75–76, 95,
104–5, 119
will of, x, 20,
26–27, 47,
53–55, 58, 75,
97, 119
González, Justo,
104–5
Gospels. *See* Bible
Gramsci, Antonio,
59
Grande, Rutilio, 63
Grant Jacquelyn, 99
grassroots, 4, 46,
66–68, 71, 76,
114, 121, 124,
134
Guatemala, 16–18,
22–23, 25, 29
guerrilla movements,
6, 24, 29, 34, 73,
142
Gutiérrez, Gustavo,
10, 34, 40,
65–66, 81–82,
142–43

Haiti, 137
han, 108, 123, 125
harmony, 54, 109,
128, 130, 136,
138–39
Hatuey, 6, 13
Hayden, Lewis, 93
heaven, 6, 19,
51–52, 108, 139
hermeneutical circle,
70–71
hermeneutics of sus-
picion, 91–92, 99
Hidalgo y Costilla,
Miguel, 15

Index

Hinduism, 4, 105, 127–32, 140

Hispanic. *See* Latina/o

Hispanic theology, 100–105

Holocaust, 120–21

Honduras, 25

hooks, bell, 92

Hopkins, Dwight, 100

hsiao, 108–9

Humanism, 4, 132–33

human rights, 24–26, 37, 81, 110

indecent theology, 147–50

institutional violence, 57, 79

Isasi-Díaz, Ada María, 105

Islam, 4, 8–9, 95, 115–19, 122, 130–31, 140

Israel, State of, 120–22

Jamaica, 137

Japan, 55, 105–6, 110–11

Jesus Christ
  abundance of life in, 1–2, 19–20, 42–45, 57
  as black, 98–99
  conversion to, 6, 8–13, 44, 51, 54, 136
  incarnation, 51, 66, 103–5
  as Indian, 13
  as liberator, 39, 51–53, 67, 71, 97–99
  as *mestizo*, 4, 103
  mission of, 8, 34, 42, 51, 53, 57, 67, 95, 121–22, 142
  suffering of, 13, 51–52, 72, 98–99, 105, 121, 124, 131, 133

John Paul I, Pope, 81

John Paul II, Pope, 60, 81, 83

John XXIII, Pope, 29, 31–32

Juan Diego, 104

Judaism, 8–9, 50, 54, 119–21

karma, 127–28

Keith, Minor, 16

Kennedy, John F, 29

Kennedy, Joseph, 24–25

King, Martin Luther, Jr., 95–98

Korea, 107–9, 123–24, 147

Koyama, Kosuke, 111–12

Krishna, 128

Kwok Pui-Lan, 146

Latina/o, 86, 100–105, 145

Latin America
  conquest of, 4–14, 16–18, 23, 28–29
  development of, 14–18, 122
  liberation theology, 4, 10, 26–27, 30, 34, 37–38, 46, 58, 65–86, 88, 92–93, 96, 100–101, 114, 134–35, 140–43, 145
  military, 2, 16, 18, 21–26, 28–29, 33, 37–39, 62, 64, 71, 74, 78
  and the United States, ix, 2, 16–18, 21–26, 28–29, 32, 37, 39, 55, 62, 64, 71, 77, 78, 81, 86, 102
  wars of independence, 15–16

Lee, Jung Young, 109

Leo XIII, 30

LGBT. *See* queer theology

liberation theology
  black, 42, 93–100
  description of, 19–20, 28, 42–61, 65, 67, 114, 150
  Hispanic, 100–105
  in Latin America 4, 10, 26–27, 30, 34, 37–38, 47, 58, 65–86, 88, 92–93, 96, 100–101, 114,

134–35, 140–43, 145
vs. liberative theology, 4, 88, 113–15
and Marx, 59–62, 75–76
Minjung, 123–25
misinformation of, ix–x, 4, 26, 41–42, 81, 83
origins of, 5–6, 10, 12, 26, 30, 37–40, 54, 64–84, 79, 119
Palestinian, 121–23
pastoral, 26–27, 46, 65, 68–69, 101, 150
philosophy of, 49, 74–75, 98, 132–33
revolutionary nature of, ix, 3, 15, 26, 33–34, 57, 70, 76–77, 80, 89, 115
and United States, ix, 16, 18, 21–26, 28, 37, 85–112
liberative theologies
African, 137–39
Buddhist, 125–27
Dalit, 130–32
Hindu, 127–31
Humanism, 132–33
Islamic, 115–19
Jewish, 119–21
vs. liberation the-

ology, 4, 84, 113–15
Native American, 134–37
non-Christian, 113–21, 125–40

MacEoin, Gary, 81
Madinah, 115
Malcolm X, 95–97
Marx, Karl, 19, 59–62
Marxism, 19, 28, 30, 39, 41–42, 59–62, 75–76, 80, 99, 118, 132, 143. *See also* communism
McAfee Brown, Robert, 87
Mecca, 115, 118
Medellín Conference, 37–39, 60, 79–80
mestizos, 15, 102–5
Mexican American Cultural Center, 101, 104
Mexico, 46, 74–76, 78, 81, 104
military
of colonizers, 8–9, 13, 16–18, 24, 60
contras, 24, 81
death squads, 22, 25, 33, 64, 71, 74
dictatorship, 18, 22, 25, 33, 37, 62, 64, 78, 141
Latin American, 24–26, 29, 33,

39, 64, 71, 78, 81
and revolutions, 15, 18, 28–30, 33–36, 59, 62, 77, 80, 142
of Spain, 13, 21–22
of United States ix, 2, 16–18, 21–26, 29, 33, 39, 62, 64, 71, 78, 81, 90
Minjung, 123–25
Miranda, José Porfirio, 75–76
Mitchem, Stephanie, 97
Moakley, Joseph, 25
Montesinos, Antonio, 9
Moors. *See* Islam
Moses, 54
Muhammad, the Prophet, 115, 117–18
mujerista, 105
multinational corporations, 16–18, 22–23, 59
Muslim. *See* Islam

narrative theology, 111
Native Americans
genocide of, 5–6, 8, 13–14
and liberative theology, 134–37
oppression of 5–15, 17, 136
people of, 6, 8, 101–2, 104, 134–36

Index

Native Americans
(*continued*)
slavery of, 6, 8–
11
neoliberalism. *See*
capitalism
nepantla, 102
Ng, David, 111
Nicaragua, 24, 81,
142
Nigeria, 137
Nirmal, Arvind P.,
131
nirvana, 126–27

Obama, Barack, 41
Obando y Bravo,
Miguel, 81
oppression
beneficiaries of x,
2, 20, 24, 50
caste, 118, 130–
32
causes of, x, 4,
19, 28, 37, 48,
57, 60–61,
145
colonialism, 2,
5–18, 24, 32,
60, 74, 95,
115, 123, 129,
134–35, 143,
145
human rights vio-
lations, 24–26,
37, 81, 110
imposition of, 2,
15, 39, 43,
113
landholders,
15–16, 31, 76,
144
patriarchy, 88–91,
93

plight of, 5, 49,
53, 60, 69
resistance of, 1–6,
9–10, 15, 26,
38, 115, 130,
135, 139–40,
146
slavery, 6, 8–11,
13, 15, 50, 54,
57, 73, 93–98,
119, 134, 137,
145
orisha, 137–40

Palestine, 113, 120–
23
Palestinian Christian
liberation theol-
ogy, 121–23
Panama, 25
Park Chung-hee, 125
Parks, Rosa, 95
patriarchy, 88–91, 93
Paul, St., 76, 91
Paul VI, Pope, 32,
35
Peru, 29, 65
Philippines, 21, 107
Pinn, Anthony B.,
132
Pius XI, Pope, 30
pluralism, 108–9,
111–12, 123–24,
146
Polycarp, 3–4
Portugal, 8
postcolonial theory,
145–47
praxis, 11, 13, 26,
28, 34, 37–38,
44, 47–51, 60,
66–67, 69–70,
90, 103, 119,
121, 123–25,

127, 130, 132,
140, 145, 147–51
preferential option,
10, 38–39, 50,
103, 115–17,
119, 145
Preston, Andrew, 16
promised land, 50,
54, 119, 121,
123, 134
prosperity theology,
145
Protestant, 6, 76–77,
103, 109–11,
121, 135, 137–
38, 145. *See also*
Christianity
Puebla Conference,
81
Puerto Rico, 21, 103

Qadoos, Izdat Said,
121
Quadragesimo Anno,
30
queer theology, 87,
97, 143, 147
Qur'an, 116–17, 119

racism, 41, 43, 51, 78,
86–87, 92, 93–
100, 106–7, 118
Ramos, Julia Elba, 73
Ratzinger, Joseph,
81–83
Reagan, Ronald, 24
Rejón, Francisco
Moreno, 46
Richard, Pablo, 15
Roberts, J. Deotis,
98–99
Roman Catholic, 3,
6–8, 10, 25,
28–35, 66–69,

71, 73, 75–83,
103–5, 114–15,
134–35, 137,
145. *See also*
Christianity *and*
Vatican
Romero, Oscar, 25,
63–64
Roosevelt, Franklin
D., 107
Roosevelt, Theodore,
16
Ruether, Rosemary,
92

salvation
of "believers,"
11–12, 32, 46,
51–54
history, 124
impediment to 2,
11, 51, 140,
144
as liberation,
11–13, 28,
43–44, 46,
51–52, 59, 72,
97, 103, 131
of non-Christians,
7–9, 13, 32,
72, 135
of oppressed, 7–8,
11–13, 20, 28,
39, 46, 72,
131
of oppressors,
11–12, 20, 72,
98
Sandinista, 81, 142
Sano, Roy, 110
Santería, 137
Santo Domingo, 10
School of the Ameri-
cas, 24–26

Second Vatican
Council, 30–33,
35, 37, 69, 79
see-judge-act, 28,
48–49, 151
Segovia, Fernando F.,
146
Segundo, Juan Luis,
69–71
sexism, 43, 51, 78,
86–93, 100, 104,
147
Shari'ati, Ali, 117–18
Shaull, Richard, 77
Sherwood, Fred,
22–23
sin, 3, 27–28, 44,
54–57, 66, 99
slavery, 6, 8–11, 13,
15, 50, 54, 57,
73, 93–98, 119,
134, 137, 145
Sobrino, Jon, 71–73,
82
social (in)justice, 11,
31, 36, 37, 39,
42, 46, 49, 53,
75, 81, 108, 118–
19, 127
socialism, 36, 38–39,
61, 76–77, 80,
89, 99, 118, 125,
141
social location,
44–48, 53, 64,
71, 92, 101, 105,
109, 143
solidarity, 2–4, 6,
9–10, 12–13, 18,
32–34, 46,
50–51, 57–58,
63–64, 66, 77,
84, 95, 97, 99,
105, 111, 119,

121, 123, 125,
127, 130
Song, Choan-Seng,
109
Soviet Union, 28–29,
39, 55, 60, 74
Spain, 5–15, 21–22,
71, 73, 137
Stanton, Elizabeth
Cady, 90–91
Stockwell, John, 24
subversive theology,
3
Sugirtharajah, R.S.,
145
Suh Nam-dong, 124
survival theology, 103
story theology, 109

Taiwan, 109
Tamez, Elsa, 78
Tanzania, 88
Taoism, 106
Thailand, 111, 113
Thich Nhat Hanh,
127
theology of revolu-
tion, 77
theology of solidarity,
121
third eye theology,
109
Thurman, Howard,
93
Tibet, 127
Tinker, George,
13–14, 135–36
Torres, Camilo, 34
Torres, Sergio, 86, 88
Trible, Phyllis, 91–92
Trinidad, 137–38
Trujillo, Alfonso
López, 79–80, 83
Truth, Sojourner, 93

Index

Tubman, Harriet, 93
Turner, Nat, 93

United Fruit Company, 16, 18
United States
  imperialism, 16–18, 21–22, 26, 74, 77
  and Latin America, 16–18, 21–26, 28–29, 33, 37, 39, 55, 62, 64, 71, 77, 78, 81, 86, 102
  and liberation theology, ix, 16, 18, 21–26, 28, 37, 85–112
  military of, ix, 2, 16–18, 21–26, 29, 33, 39, 62, 64, 71, 78, 81, 90
  and multinational corporation, 16–18, 23, 39, 55
  wars, 21–22, 24, 26, 81, 90, 107, 110–11
Upanishads, 128
Uruguay, 39, 69

Vatican, 7, 30–33, 35, 37, 67, 69, 73, 79, 82
Vedas, 128
Vekeman, Roger, 79–80
Venezuela, 29, 137
Vietnam, 127
Virgin of Guadalupe, 104
Voudou, 137

Walker, Alice, 97
Wallace, Chris, 41
Ward, Samuel Ringgold, 93
Warrior, Robert Allen, 135
West, Cornel, 99
Western Hemisphere Institute for Security Cooperation (WHISC). *See* School of the Americas
Whipple, Henry Benjamin, 135
womanist theology, 97, 99
World Council of Churches, 76, 147
worship, 27, 31, 51, 93–95, 105, 108–9, 116, 118, 130, 137

Yoruba, 137–39
Young Christian Workers, 48

Zionism, 120, 122–23